GREAT COLOR & PATTERN COLLECTION

WITH

BETSY SPEERT

MEREDITH BOOKS
DES MOINES, IOWA

Great Color & Pattern Collection with Betsy Speert
Contributing Writer: Melissa Bigner
Contributing Graphic Designer: Sundie Ruppert, Studio G
Assistant Art Director: Erin Burns
Copy Chief: Terri Fredrickson
Publishing Operations Manager: Karen Schirm
Senior Editor, Asset & Information Management: Phillip Morgan
Edit and Design Production Coordinator: Mary Lee Gavin
Editorial Assistant: Kaye Chabot
Book Production Managers: Pam Kvitne, Marjorie J. Schenkelberg,
  Rick von Holdt, Mark Weaver
Contributing Copy Editor: Jane Woychick
Contributing Proofreaders: Julie Collins, Sue Fetters, Jeanée Ledoux
Cover Photographer: William Stites
Contributing Indexer: Sharon Duffy

Meredith® Books
Executive Director, Editorial: Gregory H. Kayko
Executive Director, Design: Matt Strelecki
Managing Editor: Amy Tincher-Durik
Executive Editor: Benjamin W. Allen
Senior Editor/Group Manager: Vicki Leigh Ingham
Senior Associate Design Director: Mick Schnepf
Marketing Product Manager: Brent Wiersma

Publisher and Editor in Chief: James D. Blume
Editorial Director: Linda Raglan Cunningham
Executive Director, New Business Development: Todd M. Davis
Executive Director, Sales: Ken Zagor
Director, Operations: George A. Susral
Director, Production: Douglas M. Johnston
Director, Marketing: Amy Nichols
Business Director: Jim Leonard

Vice President and General Manager: Douglas J. Guendel

Meredith Publishing Group
President: Jack Griffin
Senior Vice President: Karla Jeffries

Meredith Corporation
Chairman of the Board: William T. Kerr
President and Chief Executive Officer: Stephen M. Lacy

In Memoriam: E.T. Meredith III (1933–2003)

All of us at Meredith® Books are dedicated to providing you with information and ideas to enhance your home. We welcome your comments and suggestions. Write to us at: Meredith Books, Home Decorating and Design Editorial Department, 1716 Locust St., Des Moines, IA 50309-3023.

TABLE OF CONTENTS

When I went off to college, though, I didn't know interior design was my passion, any more than I knew it was an actual profession or even a major. I studied theater, and after graduation, a boyfriend commented that I was always rearranging our friends' living rooms. He suggested I look into interior decorating, and when I signed up for a class, everything suddenly clicked. Design covered so much that appealed to me: drafting, space planning, architectural detail, lighting ... I'd found my dream career.

After I got my decorating degree, I interned and worked in the greater Boston area. When I went out on my own, I made my reputation on my love of color and pattern and on the comfortable, pretty, unpretentious rooms I create. More than 25 years later, I'm still exploring that classic style—comfort is timeless, after all. Still, I wouldn't necessarily say that you can spot a room I've done and say, "That's a Betsy Speert room," because ultimately, I design for my clients. And since everybody needs different things to make them feel at home, every house ends up being singular. Interior design is very personal that way.

And that brings me to why I've written this book: It's my way of coaching you to create your own singular space with gorgeous colors and classic patterns. On these pages, I'll help you analyze what elements make you feel at home, because that's the purpose of your house. I'll walk you through my stage-by-stage approach to decorating, and then I'll give you a tour of some of my favorite rooms. (Some are those I've designed for myself or clients, and others are ones I wish I'd done!) I'll explain what works in each room and give you tips and insights to create similar looks. In the end, you'll have a better feel for how to work with color and pattern to create the best thing I know: a cozy, beautiful home.

Betsy Speert

WELCOME HOME

I love it when I step into a room and am enveloped in pattern and wrapped in color. When that happens, it feels like I've been hugged, and in my mind, that's what makes a house a home. I couldn't live without that feeling or without such surroundings any more than I could live without breathing. As for how that came to be, well, I suppose it started with my childhood home.

The youngest of five, I lived with my family in an old farmhouse in a small suburb just an hour north of Manhattan. It was filled with a mix of fine and primitive American antiques, and there was a lot of pretty (and practical) wool upholstery. When summer came, my mother would cover the sofas and chairs with cotton slipcovers and take down the draperies for a bare, clean look that made sense with the season's open windows. When fall came, the draperies would go back up and the slipcovers would come off again, just in time for the fireplace to be lit. If a piece of upholstery wore out, it was subtly recovered with as similar a fabric as possible; my mother even took a weaving course and made the replacement fabric for the club chairs in our living room.

At that time I had no idea my mother had used an interior designer; the decor was established before I showed up on the scene, and in those days, people didn't discuss whether they worked with professionals or not. It turns out that she used the same firm that designed her parents' elegant Upper East Side co-op, so consequently, I was surrounded—at home and at my grandparents'—by really good examples of space planning, fabric selection, and furniture. It definitely rubbed off on me.

{ 1 Getting Started

DESIGN YOUR DREAM DECOR

I start every new design project by giving my clients a two-part homework assignment. The first half is to look through books and decorating magazines for rooms they love and rooms they hate. This book is loaded with a wide range of styles, patterns, and palettes that should give you more than enough to respond to. Pick what makes you feel good and what makes you feel rotten, what you like and what you don't like, and mark each with a sticky note.

Before you rush into the assignment, however, prepare to be surprised: Lots of people think they innately know what's going to make them feel good, but that isn't always the case. For instance, so many of us are brainwashed into thinking clutter is bad, and then we do the exercise I've described and find out that clutter is exactly what we need in order to feel at home! It turns out that one person's clutter is another person's cozy collection. Others peg themselves as pattern-haters but then choose favorite rooms that are loaded with pattern. In the end, your marked-up dream-room pages tell you what mood, feeling, and style to aim for, and what to avoid.

The second part of your homework assignment is a practical one: Think about how the space will be used and ask yourself, what is its intended purpose? Is the room a kitchen, a dining room, a bedroom, an office? What do you need to be able to do there? Eat, sleep, work, relax, or watch TV? Make note of your bottom-line goals and then move on to the next stage.

"DESIGN IS LIKE A THREE-DIMENSIONAL PIECE OF ART THAT YOU LIVE IN."

stage 1
SKETCH OUT YOUR FLOOR PLAN

After your homework is done, measure the room and create a floor plan based on the dimensions. A floor plan is the bare-bones skeleton of the room, a bird's-eye view of its walls, its windows and doors, and elements such as built-in cabinets and closets. Draw your floor plan on graph paper to make sure the outline is to scale, meaning what's on paper is proportional to what's actually in the room. I generally draft plans at quarter-inch scale (¼ inch on paper equaling 1 foot in real life) unless I'm doing a kitchen or a bath; in that case, I draw the plan at ½-inch scale.

SORT, SHOP, AND PLACE YOUR FURNITURE

Now that you have the empty floor plan, it's time to fill it up with furniture. While deciding what existing pieces to keep, remember that you want to create a place that's comfortable and functional, not a warehouse for memories. That means that sometimes you have to say goodbye to something for good, put it in storage, or stick it in another room because you can't always make what you already have work. I'm not saying you have to toss out everything old; I'm just saying you need to be selective.

At this stage ignore the fabrics and patterns of the upholstered pieces. You can either re-cover or slipcover them, or you might actually be able to work with them as they are. For now focus instead on silhouettes, shapes, and function— what each item does for your goals for the room. Also check that everything is comfortable: Everybody sits differently and everybody is a different size, so consider whether those using the room will feel at home.

If the furniture you end up with creates a complicated puzzle—too complicated or too cumbersome to actually move around the room to test out new locations—measure each item and draw its shape as seen from above to the same scale as your floor plan. Cut out these pieces and slide the paper furniture around the floor plan to find its best spot. This helps you work the keepers into your new design, delete the overflow, and see where you have holes or furniture needs. If you are short on any items (a side table, a chair, a floor lamp, anything), go shopping and mix secondhand and antique store finds with new pieces for a timeless look.

OPPOSITE MAXIMIZE SPACE BY CREATING A ROOM WITHIN A ROOM. THE RUG DEFINES THE BORDERS OF A MINI ROOM; ANOTHER GROUP OF CHAIRS AND TABLES DEFINES THE TRAFFIC PATH BESIDE IT.

RIGHT A PERFECTLY EDITED SETTING CONTAINS JUST WHAT YOU NEED AND NO MORE.

stage 3
ADD ARCHITECTURAL DETAILS

Architectural details are the fixed elements of a room that are part of its bone structure. They include functional items, such as cabinetry and counters, and decorative items, such as molding and trim. Thanks to their silhouettes, all of these add to the pattern in a room. So after you've mapped out your floor plan and filled it with furniture, consider what major details—if any—need to be added to achieve the dream look.

On the practical side, do you need more storage room or display shelving? Bookcases can be added if you have at least one foot between the wall and the path for traffic. Do you have blank spots here and there that are too odd or too tight to fit freestanding furniture? Maybe the spot is perfect for a window seat. Fill in the necessary built-ins on your floor plan, and then think about dressing the space with secondary, superficial architectural details that add more to the style of the room than to its functionality.

These secondary finishing details really make a room. I've taken a plain box of a house and turned it into something amazing by adding decorative molding alone. Before you start adding architectural details just for the sake of embellishment, take your furniture arrangement into consideration. For example, if you've arranged dining room furniture in a way that creates a lot of bare walls, I'd add wainscoting or faux paneling. But if the furniture lines the walls (and thus covers them up), there's no reason to waste your time and money with the paneling. Instead, you might add a simple chair rail or tack an interesting header over a door lintel. All of these extras—functional and form-based alike—add texture to a space and become part of the pattern that fills the room.

OPPOSITE WAXED
PINE SHELVING AND
AN ARCHED DOOR
FRAME CREATE SUBTLE
PATTERN AGAINST
ROUGH STONE WALLS.
THE ARCHITECTURAL
ELEMENTS ALSO
REINFORCE THE NEUTRAL
COLOR SCHEME.

LEFT WORK IN A DISPLAY
SHELF BY ADDING A
DOOR HEADER. THE
HEADER HERE SUCCEEDS
BECAUSE THE EXISTING
MOLDING IS SIMILARLY
SUBSTANTIAL; THE
HEADER'S SILHOUETTE
ECHOES THE SHAPE OF
THE FIREPLACE MANTEL
IN THE FAR ROOM.

I dive into patterns by choosing a primary fabric. Calling it "primary" doesn't necessarily mean it's a fabric that I'll use a lot; it's just the jumping-off point for the room. I might end up with only a toss pillow or two in this pattern, but it's the one that sets the tone for the colors and scales of the other fabrics I use throughout the space. And here's a tip: Choose your primary pattern because it evokes the feeling you want for the room, not just because you like it.

Look for material in fabrics stores, furniture stores, or design centers where they have big racks of fabrics for you to flip through. Get large, loose samples when you can, so you can see the full pattern and how it repeats. If the store has fluorescent lights, or some other lighting that's unlike what you have at home, ask to take the fabric—either a sample of it or the whole bolt—outside. If you look at the colors under store light instead of natural light, the fabric won't look the same when you get it home.

Once you settle on your primary pattern, shop for solid-color fabric that will work with it, and then look for plaids, stripes, and other patterns that complement it as well. At this point grab anything that even remotely works, because the best strategy is to get a whole bunch of samples to take home. When you have a bagful, head to your house and pin (or tape) the primary fabric to the middle of an upright board. Next, tack up the other fabrics that look best with it. Keep stepping back to see how everything works together, and narrow down your selection to one, two, or three patterns in the predominant colors. Don't worry about how you're going to use all of them yet—you're just trying to find fabrics that actually complement the primary pattern and don't clash in color or scale.

Speaking of scale, that means how large or small the patterns are on a material. Here's an easy way to balance varying scales: If you have a large-scale floral as your primary fabric, pair it with a small-scale plaid. If you have a large-scale plaid as your primary fabric, choose a small-scale floral. With stripes the scale is less important, so you have more leeway. The main thing is to let the primary fabric

OPPOSITE IF ONE PATTERN IS GOOD, FIVE ARE EVEN BETTER, AS LONG AS THE COLORS ARE ALL IN THE SAME FAMILY.

ABOVE USING TWO LARGE-SCALE FLORALS BREAKS THE RULE OF VARYING SCALE. IT WORKS BECAUSE THE COLOR DISTRIBUTION IN THE TWO FABRICS IS UNEQUAL, SO THE DRAPERIES, WHICH HAVE MORE BLUE, SEEM TO HAVE GREATER WEIGHT.

pattern lead the way to other patterns. (I'll give more specific examples of great pairings in the pattern chapter.)

After you've settled on your core collection of fabrics, figure out which fabric goes where. Place the samples on the floor (or the piece of furniture) where they might end up, pretending that this is the sofa, and these are the two club chairs, and these are the draperies, and so on, to see how everything looks together. This is the best way to see if something will actually work, because honestly, there is no exact do-and-don't formula. Creating a room you like is inevitably subjective, so the only guiding rule I'll leave you with is to aim for balance. Clumping all similar patterns in one corner of the room weighs it down on one end, whereas mixing patterns around the room creates a rhythm. If you need help on this point, study the photos in this book.

stage 5
COVER YOUR WALLS WITH COLOR

The best way to choose your wall colors and wallcoverings—whether paint, wallpaper, or fabric—is to coordinate them with your primary fabric. Sometimes the main colors are really obvious, but if you can't figure it out, put the fabric on the back of a chair and step away from it. What are the first colors to jump out at you? Those are your dominant colors.

If you don't like all the dominant colors in the fabric, pick just one and choose a neutral to go with it. Here's how that works: Say it's a pattern with a lot of reds and greens and you don't like that team. Either pull out the red or pull out the green and pair it with a cream or a white. Sounds pretty, doesn't it?

Once you've sorted out the dominant colors, think back to your homework, back to the original intent of the design and the mood you're after. Keep this in mind as you pick the base wall color and its tone—my term for how deep or rich, dark or light a shade of color is. If you want to make an airy-feeling room, choose one of the lighter colors in your pattern for the wall color. If you want a cozy, intimate nest, use one of the darker colors in the primary fabric. If you happen to be a wallpaper fanatic like me—I wallpaper every wall I can get my hands on—consider your background color as the base color, and the print on it as one more pattern to work in. As for wallpaper ideas, take your cues from the loads of examples on the pages of this book. If you want fabric-covered walls, choose a predominant fabric from the room and have it backed with a sizing to hang like wallpaper. Or simply staple untreated fabric to the walls (see pages 50–51 and 198 for examples).

Personally, I can't choose a paint color until I've tried it in the room I'm working on. That's because colors change so much in the light, especially a color like eggplant, which goes from being purple in the morning to brown at night. Every color changes, and there's no way to predict how unless you put it on the wall. So buy little samples of paint and test out the colors in different areas in a room to determine the single color you like the most. Then hold your fabrics up to the color to see if the combination works.

The pictures, plates, artwork, and other items you'll hang should also play into your wall color choices. Choose a color

OPPOSITE Choose
a color from your
fabrics and cover
the walls in it. Green
creates a peppy mood
in this bedroom.

ABOVE Furnishings
can motivate your
color choice. This
chinoiserie chest
inspired the bold
China-red walls.

that will make a great backdrop. If you hang a series of painted white frames on a dark wall, for instance, those frames are really going to pop. By contrast, if you have a lot of white plates on a white wall, you'll get a soft, pretty, monochromatic look. So again go back to the mood you're trying to achieve, and choose what you want to play up or down.

Who makes the rules about which colors go together? When I was a teenager, I was told that blue didn't go with yellow, so you shouldn't wear them together. That's ridiculous! When I started making my own decisions, I would hold things up and say to myself, does that look good together or does that look bad? That I was asking myself is the important part. There aren't any steadfast rules about matching; there are only guides to what might work well together. So look at the pictures in this book and read my suggestions for pairings to find color schemes you like. Let your own pattern choices and their primary colors show you the way to combinations that make you feel comfortable.

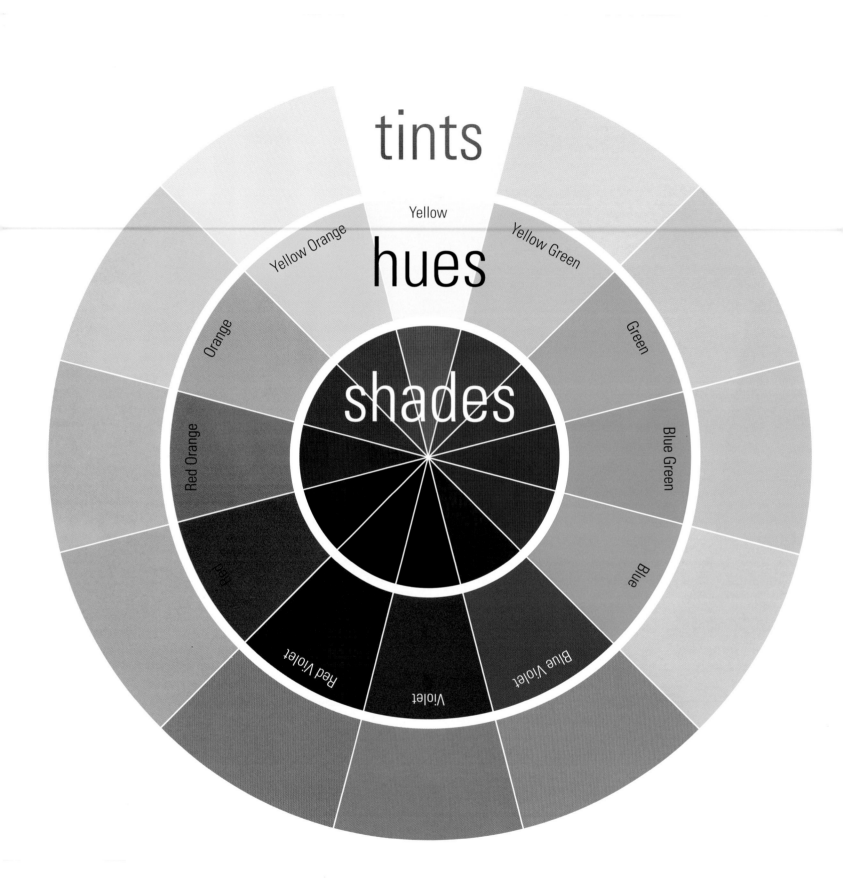

tints

hues

shades

Yellow

Yellow Orange

Yellow Green

Orange

Green

Red Orange

Blue Green

Red

Blue

Red Violet

Blue Violet

Violet

USE THE COLOR WHEEL AS A TOOL

The color wheel helps you analyze colors. Knowing its basics and how a color changes from light to dark can help you decide if two similarly colored fabrics work well together, or if a paint color complements your favorite rug. Hang in there with me for a moment, and you'll see what I mean.

The color wheel has three primary colors: red, yellow, and blue. Look at the wheel on the opposite page and focus on blue. As you creep toward the yellow portion of the wheel, you see the blue starts looking a little bit green. Eventually the color evolves into turquoise, so one way to describe turquoise is to say it's a blue with a lot of yellow in it. On the other side, when the blue starts going toward the red on the wheel, it inches into colors that are purple and periwinkle. In those cases you can say that those blues have a lot of red in them.

Thus when you look at two blues and can see that they aren't working together, you can use the color wheel to tell if there's more yellow in one or more red in another. And that can lead you to finding a better color that will pair up nicely. Think about it in terms of clothes: Black on black—how can that not go together? Have you ever tried to pair a black top and bottom and noticed that one was more blue and the other more red? That's because black actually includes every color, and sometimes more of some than others. So if you want your blacks to match (or at least complement each other), team blue-blacks with blue-blacks and red-blacks with red-blacks.

The wheel is also a good tool if you're trying to shop for colors and you've left your paint chips or fabric samples at home. Say you're hunting for furniture or linens and you don't have any of your room materials with you. When that happens—and it will—ask yourself where the at-home colors fall on the color wheel. Looking at colors this way should help you remember if something is a green-blue or a violet-blue. You'll be amazed how much you can remember and how much the color wheel can help simplify decorating.

OPPOSITE Analyze where your prints and paint colors fall on the color wheel and you'll be able to create a coordinating palette for any space. Stay within the same related hues or families (red, red-orange, or red-violet, for instance) to mix and match shades with harmony.

COMPLEMENTARY COLORS

In addition to the primary colors of red, yellow, and blue, there are three secondary colors—green, purple (violet), and orange. The secondary colors come about when the primary colors are blended together. For example, if you mix blue and yellow together, you get green; if you mix blue and red, you get purple; and if you mix yellow and red, you get orange. Look again at the wheel on page 18 and you can see that you have 12 main colors, including the primary and secondary ones. Notice that directly across from blue is orange. This pair (like yellow and purple or red and green) is a complementary color scheme.

Saying colors are complementary doesn't mean they necessarily work well together. Some of these color schemes are grating (like blue and orange), but other pairs are really pretty together. I happen to love yellow and violet, but not a strong yellow and purple, because that attracts and then repels you. So I skip the strong version and choose the same colors in soft tints, like a lilac and a sunshiny yellow. I could live with that pairing forever! The same goes for red and green. Too strong and it's Ho, Ho, Ho all year long. Lighten up the colors, though, and you'll have pink and green—a great combination. So remember that two strong complementary colors of equal value usually will be jarring, but change the intensity or strength of each and you get pretty.

OPPOSITE By
PRESENTING RED AND
GREEN AS CRIMSON
AND SPRUCE, THE PRINT
THAT'S ON BOTH OF THESE
SOFAS MAKES THE MOST
OF A COMPLEMENTARY
COLOR SCHEME. NOTICE
HOW THE BACKGROUND
COLOR CREATES TWO
TOTALLY DIFFERENT
SPACES. THE FAMILY
ROOM HAS AN INFORMAL
AMBIENCE WITH A CREAM
BACKGROUND, WHILE THE
LIVING ROOM GOES HIGH-
END AND FORMAL WITH
DEEP RED WALLS. IN EACH
CASE THE PAINT COLOR
WAS DRAWN FROM THE
FLORAL MATERIAL.

RIGHT TWEAK
RED AND GREEN TO
MAGENTA AND LIME AND
SUDDENLY YOU HAVE THE
TROPICS. RETRO-CHIC
FURNISHINGS—BAMBOO
FURNITURE, A SAUCY
LAMP, AND VINTAGE
POTTERY—TURN
THE CONVENTIONAL
COMPLEMENTS INTO
FLORIDA FUN.

{2 Color

PICK YOUR PALETTE

Everyone is viscerally attracted to one or two colors. It's not an intellectual decision; it's a gut reaction. So the most important thing you can do when you pick out your house colors is to divorce yourself from what's trendy and what's going to impress your neighbors, and focus instead on what's going to make your space your home. To get there take a look at the photos in this chapter and think about which rooms you relate to and which ones feel good to you. That will help you land in the right color family.

Once you nail down your favorite color family (your primary print or pattern might lead the way), think about function and what you want your colors to do for you. Need to make a large space cozy? Choose a dark, saturated hue. Need to make a small space feel expansive? Go for lighter tints. And if you're in a gray, foggy area and want to welcome in the sunshine, opt for warm tones from the sun—reds, oranges, and yellows. On the flipside, if you're in a hot climate, cool tones like watery blues and icy whites can lower the temperature. When in doubt, flip back to the overview chapter for step-by-step advice on color choices, and head outside for cues—after all, nature offers the überpalette.

Because this book has a finite number of pages, I've narrowed down the infinite world of color into eight basic categories: red, blue, green, yellow, brown, neutral, white, and black. When you pair up these colors, know that there are no "wrong" combinations—it just depends on how you use them. Sometimes a jarring pair of the same value works when one dominates and the other is used as an accent for little bits of punch around a room—trim on a pillow, frames on a wall, a shade on a lamp, and so on. Sometimes it works when one color is the headliner and the second is a lighter version of the pure hue. As long as you create visual balance in a room and as long as the result makes you feel good, anything goes. So have at it, and have fun at it!

"PICK COLORS THAT YOU CAN LIVE WITH HAPPILY—IT'S AS SIMPLE AS THAT."

{Red

In color talk, there's light blue, light green, light brown, and so on, but have you ever heard of a light red? Nope. That's because there's no such thing as a wimpy red. Light red is called pink, a version of red so singular it needs its own name. You can do a soft, sweet pink, but you just can't do a soft, sweet red.

Semantics aside, I like using deep reds (those on the orange side of the color wheel) in cold or foggy climates, because you walk into a room infused with those colors and immediately feel warmer. If a storm is blowing outside, you can light a fire in your fireplace and say "Let it rage," because you're snuggled down safe in your red room. If you're in a place where it's nearly 100 degrees and humid and you're determined to use red, cut it with a lot of white and it's as cool as a candy cane. Or you can lean toward the purple side of the red family for less intense rose reds, which also have a

TO WARM UP THIS NEW ENGLAND HOUSE, MY CLIENTS AND I CHOSE A SOOTHING RED PALETTE. IN THE LIVING ROOM, I WAS INSPIRED BY THE CRIMSON ROSES IN THE AUBUSSON RUG AND CREATED THE SCHEME AROUND THEM.

cooling effect. I have done true reds in summer rooms, but I tend to incorporate them on the furniture rather than on the walls to keep the space crisp, clean, and airy.

In the realm of fabrics, red is a headliner. Remember how I told you how to analyze fabric? Lay it against a chair and step back; the colors that pop out at you are the ones to pull out of the fabric and work in around the room. Give that a try and you'll notice that even if there's not a lot of red throughout a pattern, it's usually one of the main colors that jumps out at you. When that's the case, you can do all your accents in red and create a red room, because red is the color that dominates the primary fabric.

As for pairings, red works especially well with yellow, white, or green. One way to team them up is to use one of the other colors on the wall as the background with red as a print upon it. Think of an ocher with a pink-red toile pattern

ABOVE AND OPPOSITE THE MEDLEY OF FABRICS USED IN THIS LIVING ROOM CREATES A COHESIVE LOOK. THE PATTERNS COEXIST PEACEFULLY BECAUSE EACH USES THE SAME SHADE OF RED.

or a white with a pink toile pattern. That's so feminine and feels so French. And you'll find unexpected success stories too, like turquoise with deep reds and olive greens with ruby reds. No matter how you spin it, surround yourself with any red and you're guaranteed instant coziness.

"RED ROOMS, EVEN IF THEY ARE ONLY SUBTLY RED, ARE ALWAYS RICH AND WARM."

LEFT SURE, THE DESIGNER OF THIS STUDY COULD HAVE PAINTED THE WALLS A LIGHTER SHADE OF RED. BUT THE RESULT WOULD HAVE BEEN NOWHERE NEAR AS RICH AS THIS ONE. GO BOLD TO CREATE A 100 PERCENT FABULOUS RED ROOM.
(Cyndie Seely, designer)

RIGHT A SUBTLE, SOPHISTICATED COLLAGE OF RED-BASED PRINTS AND PATTERNS IS BEHIND THE WARM FEELING OF THIS RELAXING RETREAT. ALTHOUGH THE REDS VARY, THE MIX SUCCEEDS BECAUSE EACH COORDINATES WITH THE SAME YELLOW THAT'S USED THROUGHOUT THE ROOM. THE BOOKSHELVES ARE COVERED IN THE VINED WALLPAPER TO BLEND WITH THE WALL. THIS IS AN EASY WAY TO ADD ELEGANCE TO A SIMPLE SHELVING SYSTEM.
(Sabine Marchal, designer)

PAGES 32–33 THE CANDY-APPLE RED WALLS OF THIS SPACE WORK BECAUSE THE COLOR IS BROKEN UP BY WALL ART AND REFLECTED IN VARIOUS FORMS—IN THE GIANT MIRROR, ON THE LAMPSHADES, ON THE LEATHER-SEATED CHAIR, AND IN A FIELD OF PRINTS.
(Scott Salvator and Michael Zabriskie, designers)

LEFT CUTTING SOLID BLOCKS OF TRUE RED WITH WHITE COOLS OFF THIS WARM, SUNNY SPOT. THE CHECKERED PILLOWS WERE FORMED BY SEWING SQUARES OF RED AND WHITE TOGETHER IN WHAT'S CALLED A COUNTERPOINT PATTERN. (JEAN CALLAN KING, DESIGNER)

OPPOSITE WRAPPING A BATH IN A TOMATO RED COLOR IS AS TOASTY AS WRAPPING YOURSELF IN A WARM, FLUFFY TOWEL. HERE THE DESIGNER CHOSE NONTRADITIONAL ACCESSORIES TO COMPLEMENT THE NONTRADITIONAL PALETTE. A MAGAZINE RACK IS REPLACED WITH LUXE BOOKSHELVES THAT ARE FILLED WITH RED LEATHER-BOUND VOLUMES, AND THE VANITY IS A CONVERTED ANTIQUE BUREAU. (ANNE GALE, DESIGNER)

"RED IS THE COLOR OF PASSION, THE COLOR OF EXCITEMENT, THE COLOR OF HEAT, THE COLOR OF OPULENCE."

MY DEFINITION OF
ENGLISH COUNTRY IS
MIXING A HODGEPODGE
OF PATTERNS THAT
WORK TOGETHER
BEAUTIFULLY. HERE'S
THE QUINTESSENTIAL
EXAMPLE, RENDERED
IN RED. THROUGH HER
ALLEGIANCE TO ONE
STRONG COLOR, THE
DESIGNER WAS ABLE TO
INCORPORATE TOILE,
PAISLEY, FLORALS, AND
STRIPES WITH HARMONY.

(LYNN VON KERSTING, DESIGNER)

LEFT AND OPPOSITE
THESE TWO VIEWS OF THE
SAME LIVING ROOM SHOW
HOW A SPACE WITH A LOT
OF RED IN IT CAN BE LIGHT
AND AIRY, EVEN WHEN IT'S
FULL OF PATTERNS AND
CHUNKY UPHOLSTERED
PIECES. THE RED FABRIC
THAT COVERS THE SOFAS
AND CHAIR INSPIRED THE
YELLOW FOR THE WALLS,
AND WHITE TRIM KEEPS
THE SCHEME FRESH AND
SUMMERY. OPEN-BACK
SIDE CHAIRS, A WHITE AND
RED CLOTH COVERING
THE COFFEE TABLE, AND A
LIGHT-COLOR SISAL
RUG BALANCE THE
VISUAL WEIGHT OF THE
WARMER HUES.

(LYNN VON KERSTING, DESIGNER)

This room is all about excess. Using three large prints is normally a no-no, but if you love the excitement of lots of pattern, use color as the unifying thread to pull them all together. Red appears in all of these fabrics, with yellow as the secondary color and doses of white for relief. I just adore how even the lampshade is covered in a floral similar to the draperies.

(Lynn von Kersting, designer)

LEFT THINK OF A GARDEN OF RED ROSES, RED GERANIUMS, RED BEGONIAS, AND EVEN RED TOMATOES AND YOU SEE WHY THE COLOR IS SUCH A NATURAL CHOICE FOR OUTDOOR DECORATING. PAIRING BOLD BURSTS OF THE COLOR WITH WHITE COOLS THINGS OFF AS MUCH AS AN ICY PEPPERMINT DOES.

(LYNN VON KERSTING, DESIGNER)

RIGHT ALTHOUGH THE WALLS ARE PALE GREEN, THE PILLOWS, CARPET, AND DRAPERIES TIP THE SCALE TO RED IN THIS ROOM. LITTLE TOUCHES, BIG IMPACT—IT DOESN'T TAKE MUCH RED TO STEAL THE SHOW. HOWEVER, YOU'LL SEE THE OTHER END OF THE ROOM ON PAGE 84 IN THE CHAPTER ON GREEN. THERE A PAIR OF PALE GREEN SLIPPER CHAIRS COMMANDS THE COLOR PALETTE. THIS ROOM ALSO ILLUSTRATES MY POINT ABOUT COMPLEMENTARY COLORS WORKING WELL TOGETHER WHEN YOU LIGHTEN THE INTENSITY OF ONE OF THEM.

(LORI SPROWS, DESIGNER)

WITH RED-PRINT
SLIPCOVERS AND
A PREDOMINANTLY
RED RUG, THIS COZY
CONVERSATIONAL
GROUP SEEMS TO
EMBRACE YOU. CREAMY
YELLOW-TONE WALLS
PICK UP THE HINT OF
OCHER IN THE RUG AND
CREATE AN ENVELOPE
OF SUNNY COLOR. THE
NEOCLASSICAL-MOTIF
FABRIC ON TWO OF THE
CHAIRS MATCHES THE
ELEGANT FORMALITY
OF THE FRENCH
OVERMANTEL MIRROR
AND DECORATIVE PAINTED
PANELS. BUT PAIRING
IT WITH OTHER RED
PRINTS PLAYS DOWN THE
FORMALITY.

(PENNY BIANCHI, DESIGNER)

LEFT LIGHTEN RED TO THE MAX AND YOU GET AN AIRY PINK, AS IN THIS ROMANTIC COTTAGE-STYLE ROOM. NOTICE HOW CASUAL COTTON SLIPCOVERS AND A CHIPPED COFFEE TABLE OFFSET SOPHISTICATED PIECES (THE MIRROR FRAME, THE URN, THE CRYSTAL CHANDELIERS). WHITE SIMILARLY COUNTERBALANCES PINK, TONING DOWN THE SWEETNESS OF THE LATTER WITH A CLEAN-SLATE CONTRAST.

(SUSIE HOLT, DESIGNER)

ABOVE CREATE DEPTH IN A MONOCHROMATIC ROOM BY CARRYING THE WALL COLOR ONTO THE UPHOLSTERY. NOTICE HOW THE SHIMMERING EFFECT OF THE MURANO GLASS MIRROR FRAMES REPEATS ON THE SILK CHAIRS.

(SUSIE HOLT, DESIGNER)

PAGES 48–49 ADD A LITTLE YELLOW TO RED AND YOU GET A WONDERFUL SHADE OF PUMPKIN. DRESSING THE WINDOWS IN THE SAME SUMPTUOUS SHADE AS THE WALLS MAKES THIS VOLUMINOUS SPACE MORE INTIMATE; IT BECOMES AN UNBROKEN ENVELOPE OF COLOR THAT SHOWS OFF THE BLACK FURNISHINGS.

(AMELIA T. HANDEGAN, DESIGNER)

49

{Blue

As a little kid I really, really loved my crayons, and when I got a giant box, I noticed there was a blue-green and a green-blue. After I colored with each, there was no doubt they were two totally different colors. That got me thinking, and I soon figured out that green-blue is a blue with green in it, and blue-green is green with blue in it. There's a huge spectrum of possibilities with blue— periwinkle, lilac, sky blue, French blue, to name just a few—and that big box of crayons was only the beginning.

When I look for tint and tone direction to spur a decorating scheme, I tend to look out the windows of the house I'm working on. When I see the ocean, it's prime time for a blue palette. In New England, where the water tends to be dark and has a red tint to it, navy and true blues are great choices. As you go farther south, the color of the water lightens up and has more green in it, which is why turquoises work so well in places like Florida. But

AT ONE TIME MATTRESS FABRIC WAS A BLUE AND WHITE STRIPED COTTON CALLED TICKING. I WRAPPED THIS ROOM IN THE MATERIAL—YOU SEE IT ON THE BUTTON-TUFTED HEADBOARD, WALLS, AND CEILING. AND IT'S MORE THAN JUST PRETTY—TICKING HIDES CRUMBLING PLASTER.

"ONE OF THE BEST FOURTH OF JULY HOLIDAYS I EVER HAD WAS WHEN I DID THIS ROOM WITH A BUNCH OF MY FRIENDS. YOU CAN PUT FABRIC ON A WALL BY YOURSELF, BUT IT'S A LOT EASIER WITH TWO OR MORE PEOPLE."

OPPOSITE THE PALE
BLUE TICKING-COVERED
WALLS MAKE A GREAT
FOIL FOR MELLOWED OIL
PAINTINGS AND ANTIQUE
FURNITURE. I PLACED
A SERVER BELOW A
LANDSCAPE SCENE TO
ACT AS A BEDROOM
BUREAU—I LOVE IT WHEN
I CAN USE PIECES LIKE
THAT IN UNEXPECTED
WAYS. THE BLUE OF THE
SLIPCOVERS IS DIFFERENT
FROM THE MUTED BLUE
OF THE TICKING; THE
COMBINATION WORKS
BECAUSE BOTH TINTS
LEAN TOWARD GRAY.

RIGHT LOTS OF
DIFFERENT BLUES APPEAR
IN THIS ROOM—ON THE
RUG, WALLS, CHAIRS, AND
PILLOWS—BUT WHEN YOU
STEP BACK, YOU SEE THEY
ALL BLEND TOGETHER.
THE FRESHLY PAINTED
FIREPLACE LOOKS GREAT
AGAINST THIS SEA OF
BLUE AND BLENDS IN WITH
THE TRIMWORK.

you don't have to have a waterfront home to get the feeling of one. All you need is a strong blue palette.

As you pull together a blue color scheme, know that a few pairings are winners every time. Blue always looks wonderful with a crisp white; maybe that's because everyone can relate to the way white clouds look across a deep blue sky. And blue and cream (a tint of white) look tremendously restful together. I love using that combination in bedrooms—I even have it in my own.

Blue also works amazingly well with yellow. Of the houses I've decorated, one of my favorites is on Martha's Vineyard. The property is surrounded by water, and there is something buttery warm about the light there. It feels great, so I brought those outside colors in. The interior blues are a clear, true, middle-of-the-color-wheel blue that recalled the sea, and the yellows mimic the sunshine. There is a clarity to that pairing that makes the house feel crisp, airy, and cozy all at once. It's gorgeous.

When it comes to picking patterns in shades of blue, I especially like simple prints, such as plaids, checks, stripes, and toiles, with blue and one other color. Blues and whites and

blues and yellows work for almost any kind of pattern, but green and blue plaids can be nice too. If a multicolor floral is a must-have, choose one in which blue dominates, or pick out a favorite blue from the pattern and play it up around the space so it's the color you most remember. As for mood, if you want a soft, peaceful color pairing, look for blues that tend slightly toward gray, like old-fashioned blue and white mattress ticking.

THE BLUE FLOWERS
IN THE WALLPAPER
LAUNCHED THE COLOR
SCHEME IN THIS ROOM.
I USED SOLID BLOCKS IN
THE SAME TINT ON THE
FLOOR, DUST RUFFLE,
AND CHAIR TO OFFSET
THE BUSY PATTERN. AT
FIRST THE HOMEOWNER
WAS RELUCTANT TO
COVER THE ROOM WITH
SUCH A POTENTIALLY
OVERWHELMING
WALLPAPER. BUT WHEN
SHE SAW HOW THE FLORAL
PATTERN MADE THE
CAVERNOUS SPACE COZY,
SHE LOVED IT.

LEFT EVERY DETAIL COUNTS: THESE HANDMADE LAMPSHADES UNDERSCORE THE BLUE THEME WITH HANDSTITCHED TRIM ALONG THE TOP AND BOTTOM EDGES. ADAPT THE LOOK FOR YOUR ROOM BY HOT-GLUING RIBBON OR OTHER TRIMS TO THE EDGES OF A PLAIN LAMPSHADE.

OPPOSITE THE MASTER BATH IS CONNECTED TO THE BEDROOM, SO THE WALLPAPER REPEATS THERE TO UNIFY THE STYLE AND COLOR SCHEME. THE OWNER WANTED BLUE TILES IN THE BATHROOM; THEY APPEAR ON THE FLOOR AS A BORDER. A HANDPAINTED FLOORCLOTH ADDS PATTERN INSIDE THE BORDER.

"BLUE CAN BE ONE OF THE MOST PEACEFUL, SOOTHING COLORS FOR A ROOM. GIVE ME A PALE BLUE ROOM WITH WHITE TRIM, AND IT'S SO PRETTY I WANT TO EAT IT UP."

LEFT THE SLIGHT TONAL CONTRAST BETWEEN THE ROBIN'S EGG WALLS AND THE CREAMY WHITE TRIM MAKES THIS ROOM UTTERLY DREAMY. NOTICE HOW THE PALE BLUE ON THE CHAIRS MELDS WITH THAT ON THE WALLS. WHITE TRIM, FURNITURE, AND WINDOW SHADES AND THE NEUTRAL RUG FADE INTO THE BACKGROUND TO LET BLUE RULE.

(CARRIE RAPHAEL, DESIGNER)

RIGHT I THINK THE RED, WHITE, AND BLUE FLORAL PRINT ON THE BED DIRECTED THE COLOR PALETTE IN THIS ROOM. THE WALLS COMMAND THE LOOK WITH A LIGHTER SHADE OF THE PRIMARY BLUE IN THE FABRIC. CREAM IS REPEATED IN THE PLATE COLLECTION AND ON THE LITTLE TABLE, WHILE TOUCHES OF RED POP UP ON THE LAMP, THE STOOL, AND SOME OF THE PILLOWS FOR A PULLED-TOGETHER LOOK.

(CHARLES FAUDREE, DESIGNER)

OPPOSITE It's easy to have bold color without a big commitment. Take a look at this all-white room that turned into a blue heaven thanks to a few elements in deep cobalt blue. Tired of the strong statement? Change it out with accessories.

(Nina Campbell, designer)

ABOVE Sometimes artwork holds the color that sets the tone for a space. Here the framed artwork and Cantonese china make this a blue room. Two solid-blue toss pillows on the white sofa reinforce the scheme and wake up the seating area.

(Thomas Bartlett, designer)

OPPOSITE TWO SOFT
COLORS—A PALE BLUE
AND A CREAM—WITH
BARELY-THERE TONAL
CONTRAST CAN BE USED
IN SEVERAL DIFFERENT
PATTERNS WITHIN THE
SAME SMALL SPACE.
HERE ALL THE PALE
BLUES SUPPORT THE MAIN
ATTRACTION, A PAINTED
METAL HEADBOARD.

(LINDA KNIGHT CARR, DESIGNER)

RIGHT SOMETIMES A
LITTLE COLOR GOES A
LONG WAY. THREE STRONG
SHOTS OF BRIGHT BLUE
IN THREE DIFFERENT
PATTERNS—A CHECK,
A ZEBRA, AND A LEAF—
INFUSE THIS BREEZY
BEDROOM WITH VERVE.

(LOUISE BROOKS, ARCHITECT)

PAGES 66–67 LOOK
AT THIS ROOM AND THEN
CLOSE YOUR EYES. WHAT
DO YOU REMEMBER? I BET
IT'S THE BLUE DETAILS.
AN ALL-WHITE ROOM
WITH VIBRANT BURSTS
OF BLUE—OR ANY OTHER
COLOR—DOES THAT. IN
THIS BEDROOM OPTING
FOR THE COLORS OF THE
SKY MAKES AN UPLIFTING,
UNFORGETTABLE NEST.

(BRAD MORASH AND JON HATTAWAY,
DESIGNERS)

LEFT No, I didn't put this image in the wrong section. Look closely at the blue rug and you can see how it's the foundation for the room. If the rug weren't there, the yellows and whites wouldn't zing the way they do. The artwork with the same strong blues reiterates this literal "bottom line" and ties the space together.

(David Anger, designer)

OPPOSITE One of my favorite color combinations is a lavender blue with a soft green like this pair. See how the rug unifies the palette? Its low-key colors inspired the wall color and the green soffit that rims the ceiling, and it even picks up the color of the wood in the table and chairs.

(Lisa Akins, designer)

{Green

Just as I like to use blues and yellows by the ocean, I love to use greens in the mountains and in lakefront cabins. It goes back to reflecting what you see outside the house: If you're surrounded by evergreens, it's only natural to bring those rich shades of green inside.

Green is more than just a rustic color choice—far from it, as a matter of fact. Dark greens, for instance, have always struck me as very formal. I've seen a room in which the designer painted all the bookshelves and woodwork a dark shade of green to create a sophisticated and rich look. That's a great example of how the tone of a room can be set by how dark a color is. For the opposite effect add yellow to true green and you'll get a spring green, a color that produces a casual, contemporary, and vibrant feeling.

TO SAVE THIS LIVING ROOM FROM BEING OVERLY SWEET AND TO ALLOW FOR A LOT OF PLAY WITH PATTERNS, I USED A NEUTRAL GREEN ON THE WALLS. THE PAINT COLOR DRAWS OUT THE GREEN IN THE FLORAL AND STRIPED FABRICS AND THE RUG.

"BECAUSE GREENS GO WELL WITH SO MANY OTHER COLORS, YOU CAN USE THEM AS A NEUTRAL BACKDROP."

IN FRONT OF THE FIREPLACE, I ADDED A YELLOW OTTOMAN TO BRIGHTEN THE OVERALL MUTED PALETTE. HERE GREEN ACTS AS A SUBTLE BACKDROP AND UNDERCURRENT: YOU SEE IT ON THE WALLS, ON THE CHAIR UPHOLSTERY AND PILLOWS, AND IN THE FRINGE AND WELTING.

Speaking of peppy greens, I have a designer-friend who found a rug he loved with a wonderful apple green background color (see page 81). He pulled the green out and repeated that color on the walls. Then he took the coral pink accent from the rug and used that as the accent throughout the room. He hung framed pictures with a lot of white matting, and the whole room comes across as extremely crisp, just like a tart apple. At night, when the only source of light is lamplight, the green appears soft. In the morning, with the shades open, the way the light hits those walls is absolutely energizing. It's interesting to see what can be accomplished with just one green.

LEFT BECAUSE I PAIRED THIS PALE GREEN WITH A RUSTY RED IN A RUSTIC PRINT AND A HOMEY BRAIDED RUG, THE GREEN TAKES ON A COUNTRY FEEL.

RIGHT THE MEDLEY OF GREENS ON THIS READING PORCH COMPLEMENTS THE VIEW OUTSIDE. AS FOR THE FISH TASSLES? I GLAZED LIGHT COVERS AND HUNG THEM AT THE POINTS OF THE WINDOW SCARVES FOR A SILLY NOD TO NATURE.

That example—coral and apple green—shows how red and green can work together. Head toward true reds and greens and you get a holiday look, but shift a little left of center and it's a dreamy combination you'll see time and again in gardens and flowers. Other classic green pairings are green and white, green and neutral, and green and brown. I'm not always wild about green and yellow—that's just me—but I have seen it work when there's a little punch of green in a yellow room or a little punch of yellow in a green room.

As for green-based patterns, I am wild about florals, and they nearly always have greens in them. Think about a flower print with big, juicy leaves. I've taken the green from such a print and used it on walls to create the perfect backdrop for a field of floral upholstered furniture. In that case a little green plaid offset the romance of the floral print and repeated the primary color without overwhelming the room.

LEFT I ALWAYS USE WALLPAPER WHEN I CAN, AND I CHOSE A DEEP GREEN PAPER FOR MY STUDY. GLIMMERING METALLIC STARS ADD LIFE AND DEPTH TO THE BACKGROUND AND REPEAT THE GOLD AND GREEN COMBINATION I USED THROUGHOUT THE GETAWAY.

RIGHT WHILE THE ACCESSORIES IN THIS ROOM HAVE HARD EDGES, THE SOFT TONES—EARTHY GREENS, WARM BROWNS, GOLDEN FRAMES, AND MELLOW PAINTINGS— CREATE AN OVERALL COZY EFFECT.

PAGES 78–79 SEE HOW DRAMATIC A ROOM CAN BE WHEN IT'S SATURATED IN ONE COLOR? THESE WALLS ARE ALL ABOUT GLAMOUR, WHILE THE LIME ACCENTS ARE PURELY PLAYFUL. BY SETTING THAT SEXY SOFA AGAINST THE DARK GREEN BACKGROUND YOU GET TO SEE ALL ITS CURVES—I LOVE IT!

(AMY HOWARD, DESIGNER)

OPPOSITE Compare this room with the one at right to see how similar colors can be used to create very different looks. Vibrant yellow-green and bright pink are contemporary and fun in this room and traditional yet fresh in the other.

(Traci Baldus, designer)

RIGHT The apple green palette of this room was inspired by its cheerful rug. Painting the frames a saturated green (rather than white) blends the artwork into the wall, while the pink chair and pillow pop against the green and make the combination exciting.

(Gary McBournie, designer)

Gray is typically a cooler color, yet if you fold it into green, you get a warm and restful space. Note how silvery accents, such as metallic lamps, frames, silk pillows, and a clock, play up the gray undertones of the green to emphasize the serene effect.

(David Dalton, designer)

LEFT COVER THE FURNITURE IN THE SAME COLOR AS THE WALLS (LIKE THIS PALE GREEN), AND YOU HAVE A GREAT CANVAS FOR OTHER COLORS AND PATTERNS. I REALLY LIKE THE WAY THE ABSTRACT PRINT ON THESE PILLOWS HARMONIZES WITH THE FLORAL DRAPERIES. (LORI SPROWS, DESIGNER)

RIGHT A LIGHT PISTACHIO GREEN PAIRED WITH WHITE SEEMS TO LOWER THE TEMPERATURE IN THIS BEDROOM. THE BOLD BLACK IRON BED CREATES A CONTRASTING, DRAMATIC FOCAL POINT AND KEEPS THE CALM LOOK FROM BECOMING A VISUAL SNOOZE. (SUSAN IFERGAN AND URSULA COLE, DESIGNERS)

"A LIGHT GREEN AND WHITE ROOM IS SO ROMANTIC, AND SO VISUALLY SOFT, IT JUST DRAWS YOU IN AND MAKES YOU WANT TO STAY AWHILE."

LEFT DARK GREEN TENDS TO BE A MASCULINE COLOR CHOICE. HOWEVER, USING IT IN A PATTERN LIKE THIS MAKES IT PALATABLE TO BOTH SEXES. TEAM IT UP WITH MANLY MAHOGANY PIECES AND ADD PILES OF SOFT LINENS AND DRAPERIES, AND EVERYBODY IS HAPPY.
(ANTHONY CATALFANO, DESIGNER)

RIGHT WHITE WALLS AND TRIM LET THE BRIGHT GREEN UPHOLSTERY TELL THE COLOR STORY IN THIS ELEGANT ROOM. THE ARCHITECTURE IS FORMAL, BUT THE CASUAL FABRICS MAKE THE FORMALITY APPROACHABLE.
(EILEEN KATHRYN BOYD, DESIGNER)

OPPOSITE PAIR BOLDLY SHAPED ANTIQUES WITH A BOLD SHADE OF YELLOW-GREEN, AND THE WHOLE ROOM BECOMES MODERN. PAINTING THE SOFFITLIKE BEAMS OVERHEAD GREEN SOLVED THE CHALLENGE OF WHERE TO END THE WALL COLOR AND START THE CEILING COLOR.

(AMANDA NISBET, DESIGNER)

RIGHT PULLING THE WARM REDS AND YELLOWS FROM THE DRAPERY FABRIC ONTO THE OTTOMAN CREATES A VIBRANT FOCAL POINT IN THIS TROPICAL-FEELING ROOM. ANCHORING THE ROOM WITH GREEN CARPET AND GREEN-CUSHIONED FURNITURE DRAWS A COOLER COLOR FROM THE DRAPERIES AND UNIFIES THE SPACE.

(JACK KREITINGER, DESIGNER)

{Yellow

Yellow can range from a rich, golden ocher to a watery, almost-not-there shade of sunshine. I use yellow all the time in rooms I design for clients; it has a wide appeal for men and women, depending on the tint you choose and how strong or neutral it is. On the sophisticated end of the spectrum, I really like to incorporate it in spaces that have a lot of natural-tone woodwork. Add in yellow-browns, and such a room is suddenly like chocolate and butter. And who can argue with that? Yum.

For the opposite effect, fill a space with sunshiny yellow accessories and furniture—toss pillows with yellow fringe and patterned upholstery with a dominant yellow element—and the room goes bright and alert. No matter which way you cut it, yellow is all about good mood.

WHEN MY CLIENT CHOSE THIS CHEERY YELLOW WALLPAPER, SHE SET THE TONE FOR THE COLOR PALETTE IN THE KITCHEN. OPTING FOR YELLOW CABINETRY AND PAINTING YELLOW ACCENTS ON THE CUSTOM-DESIGNED ISLAND GAVE THE SPACE A LOOK OF CLASSIC AMERICANA.

90

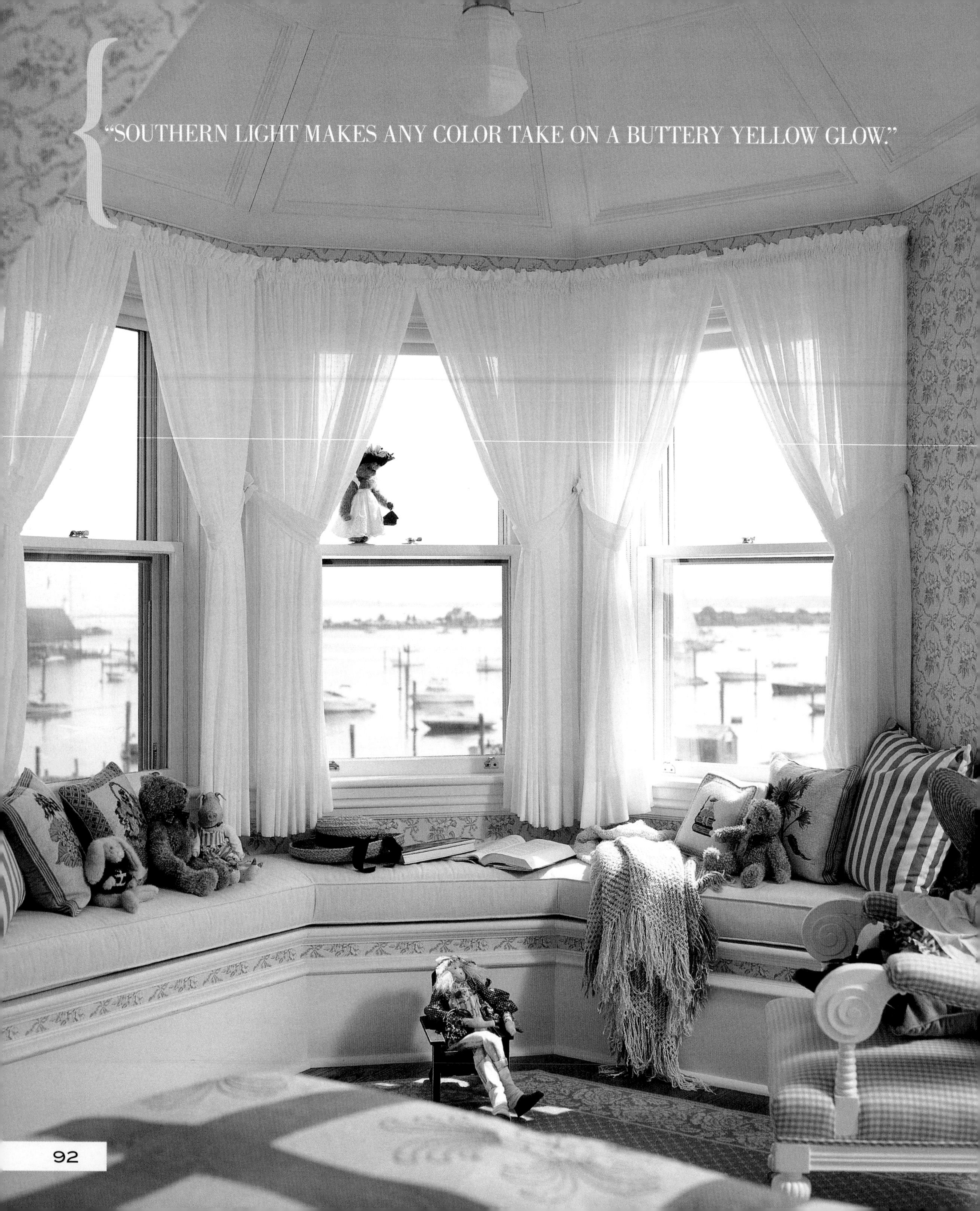

"SOUTHERN LIGHT MAKES ANY COLOR TAKE ON A BUTTERY YELLOW GLOW."

OPPOSITE TO GIVE THIS
ROOM A YEAR-ROUND
SUMMERY FEEL, I INFUSED
IT WITH SUNSHINE YELLOW
AND SEAWATER BLUE.

ABOVE WHEN YOU
USE TWO PRIMARY
COLORS—HERE A FAIRLY
TRUE YELLOW AND PURE
COBALT BLUE—YOU
GET AN ENERGETIC
COMBINATION THAT
WAKES YOU UP. WHITE
FRAMES THE ACTION AND
AMPLIFIES THE MOOD.

For one of my favorite pairings, put a strong, lemony yellow together with white. Something about those two always lifts my spirits. It's a great country look, and you don't have to be in the country to get it. Rooms like this feel so sunny that if you were in a bad mood and you curled up on the chaise in the corner… I don't see how you could possibly stay depressed. That's what yellow can do for you.

Blue and yellow is another classic color scheme that never gets old. A soft yellow and a true blue, such as a seaside blue, are so pretty, especially when you cut the combination with white accents, trim, and furniture. It's a wonderful color scheme for any country home, particularly one that is on the water, because the light is so lush and luminous there.

Checks, florals, plaids, and a great toile all do well in such a palette. And along with true middle-range blue, pretty much any other blue tint goes well with yellow. Blues on the red side, such as periwinkle and blue-violet, are especially nice with soft yellows, just as blues with a lot of green, such as turquoise, are great with bright yellows and ochers.

Always rich and pleasing to the eye, gold is one of the more interesting shades of yellow. Infuse a space with golden tones—such as brass or gold leaf—and you've warmed up the ambience without actually adding any color by way of fabric, paint, or wallcovering. Sneaky, huh?

LEFT THIS NEW ENGLAND KITCHEN NEEDED A BASE WALL COLOR TO WARM IT UP DURING THE COLD MONTHS AND ONE THAT WOULD TIE TOGETHER THE WOOD-AND-BLACK CHECKED FLOOR AND COOL WHITE CABINETS. A YELLOW WITH A TINY BIT OF BROWN IN IT WAS THE PERFECT SOLUTION.

RIGHT THE SAME YELLOW CARRIES INTO THE ADJOINING BREAKFAST NOOK, LINKING THE RICH JEWEL TONES OF THE UPHOLSTERY TO THE HONEY-COLOR TABLETOP.

LEFT Gilt frames work well in this room because they pick up the yellows in the fabric. I like the way the botanical prints pick up nearly the same colors in the floral too.

(Skip Sroka, designer)

ABOVE To get this simple and elegant look, cover your floor and upholstered furniture in white; then paint the walls that same shade. A rich yellow for windows and accessories gives the room an overall yellow personality.

(Mary Douglas Drysdale, designer)

LEFT FRENCH DISHES FROM THE 1940S MAKE A SUMPTUOUS SPLASH OF AQUA AGAINST THE MUTED MUSTARD TONES OF THIS ROOM. IT'S A PAIRING THAT EVOKES A COUNTRY FRENCH PALETTE.
(LYNN VON KERSTING, DESIGNER)

OPPOSITE WHEN YOU PUT ANTIQUE FURNITURE, ACCESSORIES, AND RUGS IN A YELLOW ROOM, THE SPACE EXUDES SOPHISTICATION AND OLD-WORLD STYLE. NOTICE THAT ALL THE COLORS HERE, INCLUDING THE FADED RED IN THE RUG, THE BLUE IN THE PORCELAIN, AND THE CREAMY WHITE OF THE TABLE, ARE OF THE SAME VALUE AS THE YELLOW ON THE WALLS. THIS MAKES FOR A QUIET HARMONY THAT LETS THE TRUMEAU MIRROR POP AS THE FOCAL POINT.
(LYNN VON KERSTING, DESIGNER)

OPPOSITE PLACING
COFFEE AND LICORICE
ACCENTS IN THIS LIGHT
YELLOW DINING ROOM
CREATES A DARK, RICH
SPACE.
(KIM ANDERSON, DESIGNER)

LEFT WHITE AND YELLOW
CREATE A LEMON-
MERINGUE LIGHTNESS IN
THIS HALLWAY. THIS SPACE
AND THE ONE OPPOSITE
SHOW THE VERSATILITY OF
YELLOW: IT CAN BE RICH
AND WARM OR LIVELY AND
CHEERFUL, DEPENDING
ON THE SHADE YOU
CHOOSE AND THE COLORS
YOU TEAM IT WITH.
(DAN CARITHERS, DESIGNER)

LEFT This monochromatic room radiates warmth thanks to its seductive, buttery color. To keep the scene engaging, the designer worked in patterns (such as the monochromatic landscape mural on the end wall and the design of the chair backs) and great details (like the fringe on the draperies). (Frederike Hecht, designer)

RIGHT Using mellow yellow in this room showcases the heirloom tapestry. The unusual choice of charcoal-blue pillows works because it echoes colors in the wall hanging. (Dan Carithers, designer)

LEFT Yellow-orange and fuchsia give this room a contemporary kick. Upholstering the wing chair in a splashy-color mod print updates and reinvents an otherwise traditional piece. (Andrew Flesher, designer)

OPPOSITE The root of this wild burst of outdoor color is almost hidden by garden greenery. Peek through the fronds to spot the ocher-painted stucco walls, and you see where the inspiration for the settee fabrics and textiles came from. (Krissa Rossbund, stylist)

106

{Brown

In my childhood home, the dining room had an elegant brown and white palette. There was brown and white wallpaper, a tweedy brown rug, white Priscilla curtains, and brown antique furniture, including a set of wooden dining chairs. It was handsome, and it was also extremely functional—with five kids eating three meals a day in there, it had to be. The absence of cushions cut down on stains, and the textured weave of the rug hid any wayward spills. Brown saved the style of that room.

Brown is that way. It's more than merely practical, it's also gorgeous and never goes out of fashion. Think about how brown looks with natural elements like wooden beams and floors, earthenware collections, stone architectural details, leather upholstery, wool tapestries, and antique rugs. Add some old, heavy furniture such as William and Mary pieces and voilà—you're in a castle! Color the walls white and work in some brown accents, then hang some gold frames, gilded

MY CLIENT WANTED TO KEEP THIS WALL COLOR, SO I BALANCED THE LIGHT TONE WITH NEW SLIPCOVERS AND DARK, TOBACCO-COLOR ANTIQUE PIECES. NOW THE SPACE IS AS LIVELY AS IT IS COZY.

{ "A BROWN ROOM IS LIKE A LITTLE BLACK DRESS: IT NEVER GOES OUT OF STYLE, IT'S ALWAYS SOPHISTICATED, AND IT LOOKS GOOD ANYWHERE."

mirrors, or brass lighting, and suddenly the look goes sophisticated. What more could you want from a color?

Because brown is actually a neutral, you can do an absolutely wonderful monochromatic room in it. (Monochromatic schemes feature one color throughout an entire room, varying it only by going lighter or darker.) There are a million variations of brown—brown that's red, brown that's green, or brown that's yellow—so stay within the same part of the spectrum for the best effect. Taupe, cream, beige, mahogany, and milk chocolate are just a few of the colors you can fold into the mix.

If a monochromatic scheme isn't for you, break up an otherwise brown room by adding small accents of red, green, or yellow throughout the space. Use the undertones of the primary brown to guide your color choices. You'll see that almost any color can look good paired with some shade of brown, and I think that goes back to nature. Have you ever seen a flower or tree that didn't look good growing up out of the dirt? I didn't think so.

OPPOSITE WOOL PAISLEY AND BROWN VELVET CREATE A PAIR OF SERIOUSLY SOPHISTICATED CHAIRS AND LINK THE COLORS IN THE PAINTING AND BRICK.

ABOVE TAKING MY CUE FROM THE WOODWORK, I CHOSE BROWN AND ROSE TEA-STAINED FABRICS AND FLOOR COVERINGS FOR THIS ENTRY HALL.

LEFT Eggplant? Brown with a wash of purple? The color of these lacquered walls defies labeling. Wrapping the walls with such a deep color takes decorating courage, but a white ceiling and light floor covering, wainscot, and furnishings keep the color in balance.

(Mario Buatta, designer)

ABOVE Sienna-tinted topographic map wallpaper, offset by the modern lines of a silver dresser and a pair of crisply upholstered chairs, gives this corner depth with an extremely chic edge.

(Charles Riley, designer)

LEFT You can invoke the elegance of brown with just a few key elements. The antique wooden table and chandelier, antique painting, and dark-stained floor tell a brown color story, even though the walls are white. The beige sisal rug moderates the dark floors, and cinnamon-color curtains add a punch of warmth.

(Greg Mewbourne, Designer)

ABOVE Brown, black, and tan make a gentlemanly color scheme that suggests old-world comfort. Brown is most apparent in the leather upholstery and wood mantel, but it also influences the yellow on the walls and the tan motifs in the chair upholstery and rug.

(Suellen Gregory, Designer)

RIGHT LOOK AT THIS ROOM AS BLOCKS OF BROWNS AGAINST A WHITE BACKDROP, AND YOU SEE A TERRIFIC COLLECTION OF SHAPES. SHARPLY CONTRASTING COLORS FOCUS ATTENTION ON THE SHAPES OF OBJECTS, SUCH AS THE WHITE CALFSKINS ON THE HONEYED FLOOR, THE FOLDED THROWS ON THE SOFA AND SETTEE, AND THE DRAMATIC CURVES OF THE ARMLESS CHAIRS.
(JUAN MONTOYA, DESIGNER)

PAGES 118–119 EVERY LAST PIECE HERE COMPLEMENTS ONE OF THE MANY BROWN TINTS FOUND IN THE STONE FIREPLACE THAT DOMINATES THIS RUSTIC DEN. THIS IS A GREAT EXAMPLE OF HOW ELEMENTS OF NATURE—STONE, WOOD, NATURAL FIBERS, AND MATERIALS—CAN ALL MELD SEAMLESSLY IN A DECORATING SCHEME.
(MARY AND GEORGE HARRINGTON, DESIGNERS)

BRING CHOCOLATE
ACCESSORIES AND
ACCENTS INTO A BLUE
SPACE AND YOU CREATE A
COSMOPOLITAN VIBE, EVEN
WHEN THE INGREDIENTS
ARE A MIX OF POP-
INSPIRED STYLES AND
CASUAL PIECES.

(DONNA TALLEY, DESIGNER)

120

OPPOSITE These bed hangings wear a bare whisper of brown that makes for a soothing nest. The coverlet and draperies feature different patterns yet share the same pale brown color. (Ardell Burchard, designer)

RIGHT As soon as chocolate brown entered this room (on the Roman shade, bolster, and silk toss pillows), it became the color to reckon with. All the other details and hues coordinate with the brown to keep the room in harmony. (Susan Jamieson, designer)

{Neutral

I can't imagine anybody walking into a room with a neutral color scheme and not feeling at home. That's because these rooms have universal appeal: They are always peaceful, very pretty, and extremely elegant. And that's why so many designers work in this palette. There's something restful about the soft environment neutrals create, and I imagine that has something to do with the nature of these colors.

Here's what I mean: To neutralize any color, throw a little brown or gray into it. Either one—brown or gray—softens the original hue and makes it less vibrant than it was before. The end color is not overwhelmingly one hue or another, and that's what being neutral means. Outside decorating terms, if a war is going on and you're neutral, you're not taking sides. The same thing goes for color. If a color is neutral, it's not really taking sides.

Take the always-in-style beige, for example. Beige is essentially white with brown in it, and because brown is basically a color stew—the main ingredients are the three primary colors, red, blue, yellow—everyone likes some version of it. I'd guess beige is so popular because it has a little of everybody in it; like a neutral country, beige can get along with everyone.

A NEUTRAL SCHEME
DOWNPLAYS THE
SHORTCOMINGS OF
THIS SPACE—A FLOOR IN
POOR CONDITION AND
A CLAUSTROPHOBIC
CEILING.

"NEUTRAL ROOMS ARE ESPECIALLY EASY TO CHANGE OUT FROM SEASON TO SEASON."

Analogies aside, if you neutralize a space the result is either a warm room or a cool room, depending upon whether you add more brown or gray, respectively. Personally, I like blues with grays in them, and I tend to be attracted to golden beiges, that is, light browns with yellow in them.

Neutrals are the closest thing to a fail-safe backdrop, because anything you put against them takes on a formal look—even junk store furniture (just put a fresh coat of white paint on it). Maybe that's why neutral spaces have always been so chic and probably always will be. They work wonders for anything that is displayed in them.

Neutral rooms also are really sharp when done monochromatically. The best ones stay in the same neutral undertone family (a range of neutrals with red undertones, for example) and use a crisp, bright white for accents and trim. To accessorize such a space, look for pieces that mimic the 1920s (gray furniture, antique-looking glass, and silver-framed mirrors), all of which work really well in cool-toned, neutral rooms. For warmer rooms, neutral greens and soft yellows are nice secondary colors. Neutral rooms work well in any part of the country and in any room in the house. Hmmm. Makes you wonder why we all can't get along so nicely.

OPPOSITE AND RIGHT THIS ADJOINING BED AND BATH SHARE THE SAME NEUTRAL SCHEME. LIGHT GRAY AND WHITE CREATE THE OVERALL SILVERY SCENE, ONE THAT IS EMPHASIZED BY MIRRORS AND CRYSTAL-HEAVY LIGHTING. MY FAVORITE NEUTRAL ROOMS HAVE A LITTLE COLOR DROPPED IN FOR CONTRAST, AND HERE YOU SEE THAT IN THE FLOWERS, ON THE BATHROOM RUG, AND IN THE TURQUOISE-TINGED CHANDELIERS.

(SUE BALMFORTH, DESIGNER)

LEFT The off-white rug in this room is woven into a textured grid whose shadows create variety. Neutrals are like chameleons, changing when light and perspectives change. (Jane Hoke, designer)

RIGHT Champagne, taupe, lichen green, cream, and gray all have their roots in the color wheel but morph into almost indefinable hues as gray and brown soften and tone them down. All the neutrals in this room are about the same value (degree of lightness or darkness), which creates a serene mood. The slightly darker note of the draperies anchors the palette. (Betty Robinson, designer)

"WHEN YOU CHOOSE ALL NEUTRAL COLORS, IT BRINGS A TREMENDOUS ELEGANCE TO ANY SPACE."

THE OPULENCE OF A
FINE TAPESTRY SETS THE
TONE FOR THIS ROOM.
EVERYTHING ELSE IN
THE SPACE IS A CREAMY
COLOR, YET THE ROOM
LOOKS RICH BECAUSE OF
THE WONDERFUL FABRIC
THAT DRAPES THE TABLE.
TRIMMING THE BOTTOM
OF THE SKIRT IN A CREAM
FRINGE LIGHTENS
THE MATERIAL WHILE
ANCHORING IT TO THE
REST OF THE NEUTRAL
PALETTE.

(MARSHALL WATSON, DESIGNER)

LEFT A NEUTRAL SCHEME PROVIDES A QUIET BACKDROP FOR A MIX OF TEXTURES AND PATTERNS. PUNCTUATING THE SCHEME WITH A FEW DARK NOTES—SUCH AS THE IRON DAYBED FRAME AND THE BROWN PATTERNED PILLOW—ANCHORS IT WITH NEEDED VISUAL WEIGHT.

(JANE FORMAN, DESIGNER)

RIGHT I THINK ANY LIGHT WOOD READS AS A NEUTRAL. BIG PANELS OF VENEERED PLYWOOD ON THE WALLS CREATE A NATURAL PALETTE OF CREAMS AND TAN. THE ORGANIC TONES ARE REPEATED ON SELECT ACCENTS, SUCH AS THE HANGING LAMPSHADE AND THE RUG. CASUAL, PALE SLIPCOVERS OFFSET THE RAW ELEGANCE.

(DOMINICK COYNE, DESIGNER)

{White

Open any magazine and there's nearly always a white room. Why? Because hands down, white rooms are some of the prettiest places you'll ever see. The trick to making them cozy—rather than sterile—is texture, pure and simple. Fill a room with a lot of soft white linens, crisp white furniture, fluffy white rugs, and filmy white draperies, and you just want to take a running jump and burrow down in the middle of that room. Really. What's prettier than a pile of freshly ironed white linens on a bed? When I do my laundry every Sunday, I iron my pillowcases so I have a few hours of nice, untouched white fabric.

Because white is its own kind of neutral, anything next to it stands out, which makes it one of the best backdrops possible. Put a piece of furniture against a white wall or hang something colorful on white, and the object's form and silhouette immediately catch your eye.

White also can be the saving grace of a piece of ordinary furniture. Here's how it works: Say you have an interestingly shaped piece, but it has a really rotten finish on it, maybe one that makes it look cheap. Slap a coat of flat white paint on the thing, and it's going to look like a million dollars. If you do a so-so paint job, it's going to look shabby chic; if you do a really good paint job, it's going to look more sophisticated than it did before. The transformation happens because you end up seeing the wonderful shape of the piece, not the shoddy old finish. This quick fix works really well on reproduction pieces from the 1930s and 1940s, a period when the finishes weren't always so great but the silhouettes were beautiful.

SUBWAY TILE, VESSEL SINKS, AND PORCELAIN-TIPPED FIXTURES COMBINE WITH MILK GLASS ACCESSORIES AND SILVER-PLATED MEXICAN MIRRORS TO CREATE A CRISP PALETTE.

"WHITE ROOMS ARE PEACEFUL, PRETTY ROOMS."

There are times when white can be practical and times when it's less so. I try to talk all my clients into doing white tile for their bathrooms and white on their cabinetry. That's because you might want to alter your color scheme in a few years, and then all you'd need to change would be the color of the walls, because white works with everything. Otherwise changing out tile is very expensive, and painting cabinets can be a pain.

Speaking of traditional looks, I like white trim everywhere; it looks good with any color. Even if I'm wallpapering a room with a print that has a creamy background, I paint the trim white instead of matching the cream. You expect to see white trim, and to me, it looks eternally clean and fresh.

I have done a fully white room before, but my clients had an incident involving a puppy, a ton of Halloween candy, and a white rug. After that, let's just say the snowy color scheme was never quite the same. Given their sad lesson, I have a warning on the practical front: If you aim for white upholstery and fabrics, get slipcovers in washable materials.

OPPOSITE THE CURTAIN THAT TELLS YOU THIS IS A FUNCTIONING SHOWER IS TUCKED OUT OF SIGHT, BUT TELLTALE CLUES ABOUND: WHITE TILES AND HIGH-GLOSS WOODWORK ARE SPLASH-PRACTICAL, AND THE IRON GARDEN CHAIR MAKES AN UNEXPECTED BUT PRETTY SHOWER SEAT.

RIGHT ALTHOUGH THERE ARE TOUCHES OF COLOR IN THIS ROOM, WHITE PAINT ON WALLS, CEILING, AND CABINETRY CREATES AN UNOBTRUSIVE FRAME FOR THE SEASIDE VIEW.

A WORLD OF WHITE
ALLOWS THIS DARK-
FRAMED SETTEE TO STAND
OUT AS THE STAR OF THE
ROOM. SOLID WHITES
DOMINATE BUT NOTICE
HOW ADDING A SUBTLE
CREAM AND WHITE STRIPE
TO THE DRAPERIES
CREATES NEEDED DEPTH.
(SUSAN JAMIESON, DESIGNER)

LEFT THIS BEDROOM (LIKE THE ONE AT RIGHT) IS AS ROMANTIC AS IT GETS THANKS TO LITTLE MORE THAN A LUXURIOUS OVERDOSE OF WHITE. SEE HOW EVEN THE PHONE ON THE SIDE TABLE IS WHITE? IN THIS LIGHT-FILLED SPACE, THE STAINED GLASS LOOKS LIKE LITTLE JEWELS.

(CAROL MARYAN, DESIGNER)

RIGHT I WOULDN'T BE SURPRISED IF THE FLAT SHEET SHOWN HERE IS ACTUALLY AN OFF-WHITE LINEN TABLECLOTH. USING TEXTILES IN OFFBEAT WAYS ADDS TEXTURE AND CHARACTER TO FURNISHINGS. LIKE THE SETTEE ON PAGES 142–143, THE IRON BED HERE TAKES CENTER STAGE AGAINST THE NEUTRAL BACKGROUND.

(MARY ANNE THOMSON, DESIGNER)

LEFT THIS RUSTIC SPACE WAS UPDATED BY COATING THE WALLS AND WOODWORK WITH WHITE PAINT. DIFFERENT STYLES OF OLD FOUND FURNITURE GET A FACELIFT WITH A COAT OF SOFT CELADON COLOR. JOINING THE TWO COLORS ON THE DUVET COVERS TIES THE ENTIRE SCHEME TOGETHER.
(NANCY DUNN, DESIGNER)

OPPOSITE THIS ROOM IS THE FLIPSIDE OF THE ONE AT LEFT. HERE THE VARIED STYLES OF FURNITURE ARE ALL PAINTED WHITE, AND THE SECOND, SOFTER COLOR IS USED ON THE WALLS AND IN THE FABRIC. BOTH ROOMS ARE EXAMPLES OF ONE-COLOR-PLUS-WHITE SCHEMES, BUT ONE ALLOWS WHITE TO DOMINATE WHILE THE OTHER PUTS MORE EMPHASIS ON THE COLOR. THE RESULT IS A SUBTLE DIFFERENCE IN MOOD.
(SUELLEN GREGORY, DESIGNER)

LEFT White walls, furniture, and accessories create a cool environment for the quintessential summer dining room. Filmy white curtains allow the sun to filter in without overheating the space. (M. E. Yeck and Robert Bouchard, designers)

RIGHT Filled with off-white elements set against a bare, honey-tone floor, this room feels extravagantly naked. The play of white on white means that shadows, textures, and subtle shifts of color take on added importance. (Charles Spada, designer)

LEFT Overstuffed, oversize upholstered white furniture is as inviting as a bed outfitted in clean linens—you want to snuggle into both. This room says take off your shoes and put up your bare feet. To comply without tarnishing the white fabrics, opt for washable slipcovers and use stain-resistant sprays.
(James Michael Howard, designer)

RIGHT Rather than fill the bookcases with an array of colorful volumes or knickknacks, the designer placed pieces of bleached coral sculpture. The shapes break up the straight lines of the cabinetry while preserving the serenity of an all-white scheme. White flowers in a white space compound the elegance.
(Charles Spada, designer)

"WHITE HAS A PURITY AND A SIMPLICITY THAT KEEP IT TIMELESS. IT NEVER GOES OUT OF STYLE."

LEFT A DASH OF RED AND BLUE IN THIS OTHERWISE WHITE ROOM GIVES THE SPACE A SLIGHTLY PATRIOTIC FEEL, AND THE QUILTS AND CHUNKY STRIPES CREATE AMERICANA STYLE. FOR A NEW LOOK, SIMPLY CHANGE OUT THE PILLOWS AND FLOWERS; A WHITE BACKDROP IS UTTERLY VERSATILE. (LOUISE BROOKS, DESIGNER)

RIGHT CREAMY HUES TAKE THIS LIVING ROOM TO THE WARM SIDE OF THE WHITE COLOR FAMILY. THE WALLS, DRAPERIES, SLIPCOVERS, AND EVEN THE OSTRICH EGGS CREATE AN AIRY ENVELOPE, WHILE TOUCHES OF GOLD AND CORAL ADD VISUAL EXCITEMENT. (CAROL MARYAN, DESIGNER)

LEFT THIS CLOUDLIKE CABANA DRAPED IN WHITE FABRIC AND FILLED WITH WHITE CUSHIONS SEEMS AS NATURAL HERE AS THE BROAD SKY ABOVE IT. POTTED PLANTS AND SMALL TOUCHES OF GREEN ON THE FURNITURE MAKE THE OUTDOOR ROOM ONE WITH THE GRASSY KNOLL. (MISSY CONNOLLY, DESIGNER)

RIGHT WHITE WICKER IS A CLASSIC CHOICE FOR GARDEN FURNITURE AND ACCESSORIES. TRUE WICKER LIKE THESE PIECES NEEDS TO BE PROTECTED FROM THE ELEMENTS. PLACE REAL WICKER FURNITURE ON COVERED PORCHES AND LOGGIAS AND DRESS IT IN WHITE SLIPCOVERED CUSHIONS FOR A COOL RETREAT THAT DEFIES SOARING TEMPERATURES. (SUE BALMFORTH, DESIGNER)

{Black

Black stops you in your tracks. It outlines, it exaggerates, it draws your eye, and when you pair it with any other color, it adds punch to the secondary color. Black and white, black and yellow, black and red, black and brown, black and lime green, black and orange—they are all fabulous, all classics. Think of a red lumberjack plaid or a yellow bumblebee, and you see what I mean.

Black has big impact so whenever it's the main attraction, you're going to have some serious drama. If you actually paint or cover the walls in black (rather than using it as an accent), you really have to know what you're doing, or you're going to end up with a room as dark as a cave. It is possible to do it well, though, and the result can be wonderful. I've never had a client request such a room, but when it happens, here's how I'll do it right without overwhelming the space with darkness.

First of all, I think the only way a black-painted room really works is when there's something light hanging on

A LITTLE BIT OF BLACK MAKES A STRONG STATEMENT AND EASILY BECOMES THE DEFINING ELEMENT IN A SPACE. HERE ELEMENTS OF BLACK MAKE THIS RETREAT CRISP AND SOPHISTICATED.

"YOU DO A BLACK ROOM NOT BECAUSE IT'S SWEET—YOU DO IT BECAUSE IT'S FABULOUS."

IF YOU DON'T WANT BLACK WALLS BUT DO WANT THE SAME DRAMATIC EFFECT, APPLY A BACKDROP OF DARK NAVY, EITHER WITH A WALLCOVERING OR WITH PAINT. EBONY-COLOR FURNISHINGS AND BLACK AND WHITE PRINTS IN BLACK FRAMES PROVIDE THE DRAMA OF BLACK WITHOUT DROWNING THE SPACE IN IT. WHITE PLAYS A KEY ROLE HERE TOO, CREATING CRISP CONTRAST TO THE NAVY AND BLACK.
(BRENDA EASTMAN AND SUSIE MITCHELL, DESIGNERS)

the walls and on the windows to soften the look and make the black act as a dramatic backdrop. I like the idea of doing this in a really small room, where I would put large light or white things—like a series of prints—on the walls. In my mind, the prints would be small images surrounded by big white mats and gold frames and would pretty much cover the wall; this would allow the black to show up as an outlining color. Then I'd hang filmy white draperies—solid white, solid white with black tape as an edging, or black and white stripes. I'd fill the room with all-white slipcovered furniture and put a lot of white pottery against the walls. That little room would be simply gorgeous!

Black also works really well as a contrast color, especially in fabric patterns. Black and white always go well together. I like white toile with black images and white with black in checks and plaids too. And lemony yellows also are really great with black in those same patterns. Each pairing works because of the strong tonal contrast and simply because if you edge anything in black, you define its shape more clearly. Black is almost like architecture, supporting any color it is paired with and making it pop.

ABOVE Black calls attention to the main attraction here: the striking windows with their graceful leaded glass and elegant lines. Framing the windows with voluminous white draperies and choosing white and neutral furnishings offsets the drama nicely.

(Beverly Balk, designer)

RIGHT This handsome sleeping alcove softens the black and white scheme with a striped half-tester (set over the head of the beds) that hangs in gentle folds. The white valance above it balances the wall of black.

(Judy Gordon and Lani Myron, designers)

LEFT BLACK AND WHITE DECOR MARRIED TO AMERICAN ANTIQUES AND FURNISHINGS MAKES A HAPPY HOME. BLACK IS A CHIC FOIL FOR PRIMITIVE STYLES.

(CHERYL STANLEY, DESIGNER)

RIGHT SELECTED PIECES OF FURNITURE PAINTED BLACK ANCHOR THIS SIDE OF THE SAME BEDROOM. NOTICE HOW LITTLE POPS OF COLOR—WHITE, YELLOW, BROWN, AND RED—GIVE THE SPACE AND PALETTE ESSENTIAL VERVE.

(CHERYL STANLEY, DESIGNER)

"I HONESTLY CAN'T THINK OF ANYTHING THAT DOESN'T LOOK GOOD WITH BLACK."

These elegant black and white striped draperies and toile linens epitomize the upscale country look. They're also bold enough to hold their own with the massive bed. I love how a framed print hangs atop the valance— it's an unexpected placement that draws your eye upward and calls attention to the generous size of the room.

(ANNE GALE, DESIGNER)

ABOVE REMEMBER
THIS ROOM FROM THE
BROWN CHAPTER (PAGES
116–117)? BLACK TABLES,
CHAIR FRAMES, AND
ACCESSORIES STAND
OUT IN SHARP CONTRAST
TO THE WHITE WALLS,
GIVING THE TRADITIONAL
ARCHITECTURE A MODERN
FEELING.

(JUAN MONTOYA, DESIGNER)

RIGHT BLOCKS OF
BLACK SHOW UP ALL
OVER THIS LIVING ROOM:
ON THE FRONT DOOR,
ON TOSS PILLOWS, ON A
COFFEE TABLE BOOK, IN
FRAMED PRINTS, AND ON
THE RUG. BLACK UNIFIES
THE CORNUCOPIA OF
TEXTURES, MATERIALS,
AND PATTERNS.

(M. E. YECK AND ROBERT BOUCHARD,
DESIGNERS)

LEFT TEAMING BLACK AND NAVY WITH BEIGE AND TAUPE CREATES A SOOTHING YET SOPHISTICATED BEDROOM. WHITE APPEARS AT CEILING HEIGHT AS WELL AS ON THE FLORAL COVERLET AND DECORATIVE PILLOW TO BRIGHTEN THE MUTED DOMINANT TONES.
(M. E. YECK AND ROBERT BOUCHARD, DESIGNERS)

OPPOSITE HELLO, STUNNING! THE STAINED FLOOR AND ACID GREEN WALLS ARE SUCH SHOWSTOPPERS THAT BLACK TAKES ON AN IMPORTANT SUPPORTING ROLE. IT CALLS OUT THE MOLDING DETAILS, FRAMES THE WINDOWS, ROOTS THE TABLE IN PLACE, AND BREAKS UP THE WALL PANELS TO CONTRAST WITH THE EXUBERANT EXPANSES OF VIVID GREEN.
(FELICITY WILDE AND KEITH IRVINE, DESIGNERS)

{3 Pattern

DRESS YOUR NEST

I bring up the word "cozy" an awful lot when I'm talking about decorating, because it's one of the main things that drives me—creating coziness. I consciously go at each room to make it as cozy and nestlike as possible, and pattern feathers a nest better than anything. Take a room, wrap it in florals or toiles (my two favorite prints), and you suddenly feel like you're being enveloped and embraced. It's the patterns—on the walls, on the furniture, in the displayed collections, and in the very room itself—that do it every time.

Ask me what constitutes a pattern, and I'll ask you to think beyond the obvious. Patterns are shapes on backgrounds as well as shapes on shapes, so in rooms patterns are captured on far more than fabric. You create pattern when you hang the same kind of object over and over again on a wall. You create pattern when you group knickknacks together on a tabletop. You create pattern when you add wainscoting or cabinetry or when you build with materials such as tile, brick, stone, and timbers, all of which bring their own shapes to the landscape of a room.

The goal in decorating with patterns is to create a space with a visual rhythm that resonates with you. This section will train you to strike that essential personal chord by learning to see patterns and how they can work together. Take a good look at the photos and read about your favorites. Beyond toile and florals, I'll cover plaids, checks, and stripes. I'll tell you about scale and mixing and matching all these patterns to design a room that sings. That's my kind of nest, my kind of cozy.

"WHEN YOU WORK PATTERN INTO A ROOM, YOU MAKE IT A PIECE OF ART."

{Toile

Toile refers to toile de Jouy, a printed cotton or linen cloth named for the French town Jouy-en-Josas, where it was first produced in the late 1700s. The cloth features scenic designs, usually printed in a single color on a light background. My favorite scenes are the bucolic ones, country settings with sheep, cows, and shepherds. When you fill a room with these gentle images, it makes for a very soft, appealing space.

It's that sensation that makes me love toile so much—so much, in fact, that I covered my entire bedroom in it. And while toile bedrooms are pretty common among pattern enthusiasts, the pattern defies being pigeonholed. Pick the right toile and it suits any space. Success depends on choosing an appropriate scene, a fabric that achieves the mood you're after (for example, silk for a formal feeling or cotton for a casual one), and a color that suits the palette of the room.

I FIRST BEGAN USING TOILE WITH THIS BLUE AND WHITE ROOM AND THE ROOMS ON THE NEXT FEW PAGES. BLUE AND WHITE TOILE IS A CLASSIC COLOR COMBO. FINISHED WITH BIEDERMEIER PIECES AND WHITE UPHOLSTERY, THE SPACE IS SPARSELY ELEGANT IN SPITE OF THE BUSY PATTERN.

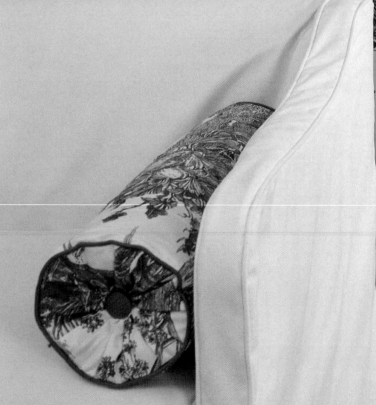

"EVEN IF IT'S PRINTED ON THE SIMPLEST OF FABRICS, TOILE IS UTTERLY SOPHISTICATED."

OPPOSITE A WALL OF TOILE IS BALANCED BY LINEAR ELEMENTS IN SOLID BLOCKS OF NEUTRAL WHITE (THE SHUTTERS, THE MANTEL, THE UPHOLSTERED FURNITURE) THAT CONTRAST WITH THE STRONG AND COLORFUL PATTERN.

RIGHT BLACK FRAMES WITH GENEROUS WHITE MATTING HELP THIS SERIES OF PRINTS STAND OUT AGAINST THE TOILE BACKGROUND AND FORM A GEOMETRIC PATTERN OF THEIR OWN.

Typically full-on toile rooms are two-color rooms. The most classic formula includes walls, draperies, and main pieces of furniture in a two-tone toile, with other accessories and furnishings sporting those same colors. To spice things up you could cover the walls with a secondary pattern in the same colors as the toile and then use toile as the primary fabric throughout the rest of the room.

A lot of designers, however, do what I call a positive and negative toile room, which means they use two toile patterns with similar designs but reverse color schemes. For example, one pattern may have a creamy white background with a colorful scene, while the other has a colorful background with a creamy white scene. It doesn't matter if they aren't exactly the same. This can be an absolutely fabulous look.

Regardless of how you pull it together, when toile is used all over a room, the space feels like an oversize hatbox.

LEFT Simple black shapes throughout the room play off the complex pattern on the walls. The cross supports under the table inspired the Xs on the pillows.

RIGHT In this room (which appears on pages 178–179 as well), light blue toile creates a mellow retreat. Using a fabric version of the wallpaper, I made slipcovers for the chair and ottoman.

Remember the old hatboxes your mom or grandmother had, with both the inside and the outside covered in wallpaper? An all-toile room is like that: When you step into the space, it's as if you're being tucked away in a perfectly wrapped box, safe and cherished. And who doesn't want that?

LEFT I USED THE SAME PRINT TO LINK THIS SITTING ROOM WITH ITS ADJOINING BEDROOM. BECAUSE THIS IS A MORE ACTIVE, PUBLIC SPACE, I ADDED CHECKS, PLAIDS, AND STRIPED TICKING UPHOLSTERY—ALL OF WHICH PAIR WELL WITH TOILE, FIGURED PRINTS, OR FLORALS—TO JAZZ THINGS UP.

RIGHT ADDING TRIM TO THE CHAIR SKIRT AND PLACING A SOLID TOSS PILLOW IN THE CHAIR HELPS DEFINE THE PIECE AND TIES IT TO THE BLUE RUG.

"I THINK BLUE TOILE BEDROOMS ARE ABSOLUTELY GORGEOUS. I LOVE DOING THEM FOR CLIENTS, AND I EVEN WRAPPED MY OWN BEDROOM IN THE PRINT."

WHEN TOILE IS CARRIED
FROM THE WALLS ONTO
THE TESTER, DRAPERIES,
HEADBOARDS, AND
FOOTBOARDS, A SIMPLE
BEDROOM BECOMES A
LUXURIOUS SLEEPING
CHAMBER.

(SUSAN SCHMIDT, DESIGNER)

LEFT A TOILE WITH SHARP TONAL CONTRAST (DARK COLOR ON A LIGHT BACKGROUND OR VICE VERSA) CREATES A CRISPER LOOK THAN A PRINT IN SOFTER TONES (SEE PAGES 180–181). TO EMPHASIZE THE EFFECT, OUTLINE THE WALLS WITH THE DARK COLOR (HERE NAVY BLUE) AND USE EXPANSES OF THE LIGHTER COLOR (WHITE) FOR VISUAL RELIEF. (MARSHALL WATSON AND CHRIS WELSH, DESIGNERS)

RIGHT TOILE EXCELS IN BOTH FORMAL AND INFORMAL SETTINGS. HERE GILT, CHINA, AND CRYSTAL ADD A LAYER OF ELEGANCE TO THIS PLAYFUL PRINT. (IT DEPICTS BALLOONING IN THE FRENCH COUNTRYSIDE.) (MARSHALL WATSON AND CHRIS WELSH, DESIGNERS)

OPPOSITE AND RIGHT THE WALLS IN EACH OF THESE ROOMS WEAR SOLID, BIG BLOCKS OF COLOR THAT ECHO CHOICE SPLASHES OF TOILE. WHILE PINK TOILE MAY HAVE BEEN THE PRIMARY FABRIC TO INSPIRE THE OVERALL PALETTE, OPPOSITE, THE VIVID WALL COLOR DOMINATES THE SPACE. AT RIGHT, OPTING FOR A SUBDUED CREAM COLOR PULLED FROM A PAIR OF SIMILAR PRINTS (THEY ARE POSITIVE AND NEGATIVE COUSINS OF EACH OTHER) LETS THE TOILE RULE. THE LESSON? BOLD COLOR CAN TRUMP PATTERN AS THE STAR OF A DESIGN SCHEME, WHILE A MORE MELLOW HUE PUSHES PATTERN TO THE FOREFRONT.

(OPPOSITE: SHEILA BARRON, DESIGNER RIGHT: LAURA MCDONALD AND CHERYL HARRIS, DESIGNERS)

LEFT COMPARE THIS ROOM TO THE ONE ABOVE TO SEE WHAT A DIFFERENCE IN MOOD YOU CAN ACHIEVE DEPENDING ON THE WALL TREATMENT YOU PAIR WITH TOILE. HERE THE TOILE DRESSES THE WINDOW, THE BED, AND THE FURNITURE, AND A TINY PRINT MAKES THE WALLS SEEM CLOSER SO THE ROOM FEELS COZIER.

(BETTY ROBINSON, DESIGNER)

ABOVE IF YOU LOVE TOILE BUT WANT AN OPEN FEELING, OPT FOR WALLS WITH SUBTLE PATTERN. HERE A SOFTLY STRIPED WALLPAPER PICKS UP THE BACKGROUND COLOR OF THE TOILE AND USES IT TO CREATE AN AIRY, QUIET ENVIRONMENT. TO ACHIEVE THE FEELING OF A TOILE SPACE, THE DESIGNER SPREAD THE PATTERN OVER ALMOST EVERYTHING EXCEPT THE WALLS.

(DAN CARITHERS, DESIGNER)

Take the mixing of toile patterns one step further and mix toile colors as well. This red toile has a blue and white print, which allows for the addition of blue toile draperies. Red and blue dominate the rug and reinforce the color scheme, while the yellow stripes add a bit of punch and contrast.

(Lori Sprows, designer)

{Floral

A lot of the chichi designers like loads of solids and grays and neutrals, but I say bah to that: Give me a pink cabbage rose pattern anytime. I don't know what it is about them, but flowers in general just make me feel good. My two absolute favorites are the most girlish ones there are: cabbage roses and floribunda roses. The first is round and fluffy and thick with several rows of petals. And floribunda? They have a single row of petals and look something like a dogwood blossom. Both are as old-fashioned and sweet as they come.

Looking through the past rooms that I've done, I can see that my love of flowers borders on obsession: I work them into a room via paintings, fabric, collectible plates, cross-stitched pillows, wallpaper, and even dish towels. But I do have my limits. First, the florals I pick have to be stylish. And they have to work in the room as far as the colors and other patterns are concerned. Last, they have to contribute to the tone I'm setting.

THIS LARGE BEDROOM INITIALLY LACKED AN INTIMATE FEELING, SO I COVERED THE WALLS IN A FLORAL PRINT, WHICH IMMEDIATELY CHANGED THE AMBIENCE. ALTHOUGH PINK DOMINATES THE PATTERN, I LED THE PALETTE WITH BLUE TO KEEP THE ROOM FROM BEING TOO SWEET.

"I'M A FLOWER GIRL—NO DOUBT ABOUT IT."

OPPOSITE THE FABRIC THAT MATCHED THIS WALLPAPER EXACTLY WAS DISCONTINUED, SO I HUNTED DOWN A PRINT THAT BLENDED WITH THE WALLS IN BOTH COLOR AND PATTERN FOR THE FURNISHINGS. THE INITIAL NEGATIVE BECAME A POSITIVE, BECAUSE THE OVERALL EFFECT IS MORE MODERN AND FRESH THANKS TO THE KISSING-COUSIN MIX.

RIGHT ANTIQUES AND LITTLE BOUQUETS OF FRESH FLOWERS UP THE ROMANCE FACTOR IN ROOMS THAT FEATURE OLD-FASHIONED FLORALS.

I say you can use florals in any room, from the bathroom to the bedroom to the kitchen. They work anywhere because there are flowery patterns that are formal and less formal, more urban or more country. The softer patterns, such as the floribunda and the cabbage roses or little nosegays of things like violets and daisies, are casual. Such patterns work well if you're going for a country or cottage look, or if you want something sweet for a girl's room. The more sophisticated and elegant florals tend to be larger-scale flowers, often mixed with classical shapes such as urns and medallions.

Folding other patterns into a floral-dominated space is easy, because flowers work with everything: plaids, stripes, toiles, polka dots, paisleys, and solids. For a winning mix pay attention to the distribution of color and pattern in the floral: Is there a lot of plain background color visible (as in the upholstery fabric, opposite), or are the flowers densely packed (as in

To complement the old pine woodwork in this Cape Cod house, I chose an orangey floral print and ended up covering both the walls and ceiling in it—a floral first for me. The "wallpaper" is actually fabric I stapled in place and then trimmed in cream gimp to hide the staples.

the wallpaper)? Note how the colors and pattern distribution of the secondary pattern complement the floral. To simplify the color scheme and pairing, I often use a floral and a two-tone plaid. Here's a simple recipe to that end.

First look at the color—the dominant, hit-you-over-the-head color—of the flower or flowers. Then look at the color of the leaves. Those two hues plus the background are the three colors you'll work with. Background, leaf, flower—it's that easy. For your secondary pattern, choose a two-tone plaid that combines the green of the leaves and the background color or one of the colors in the flowers. In other words, choose a green and white plaid if white is the background, or a green and pink, or a green and blue, or a green and yellow plaid, depending on the colors in the flowers. Then choose the color

"IF THERE'S A WAY TO PUT A FLORAL PATTERN
IN A ROOM, I'LL GET IT IN THERE."

LEFT SOMETIMES WHEN I WRAP WALLS IN A SINGLE ACTIVE PATTERN, I LIKE TO INTERRUPT THE LANDSCAPE WITH LARGE BLOCKS OF SOLID COLOR. I DID THAT HERE USING CREAMY, SHEER BED HANGINGS. THE PLAIN BACKDROP HELPS THE HANDPAINTED HEADBOARDS AND FRAMED ARTWORK STAND OUT SO THAT THEY EMPHASIZE THE BEDS AS FOCAL POINTS.

RIGHT I COVERED THIS CHAIR IN EXACTLY THE SAME FLORAL PRINT AS I USED ON THE WALLS. THIS BRINGS THE PATTERN OUT INTO THE ROOM. NOTICE HOW THE BOUQUETS ARE PERFECTLY CENTERED ON THE CHAIR BACK AND ON THE SEAT CUSHION— THAT'S HOW A GOOD UPHOLSTERER FRAMES A LARGE-SCALE PATTERN.

in the flowers that really jumps out at you and dress the rest of the room with it. Break it down like this and you'll have a primary pattern (the floral), a secondary pattern (the plaid), and a primary color (for solids, accents, and paint choices). Instant floral room, instant heaven.

OPPOSITE WHEN I FIRST DECORATED THIS ROOM IN MY OLD LAKE CABIN, I COULDN'T AFFORD TO PUT UP DRYWALL, SO I HID THE BARE WALLS BY STAPLING UP BEDSHEETS. THE OLD PAPER LAMPSHADES WERE A TERRIFIC JUNK STORE FIND AND REPEATED THE FLORAL MOTIF.

RIGHT IT STILL AMAZES ME HOW THIS ONE SHOWER CURTAIN TRANSFORMED MY LITTLE MASTER BATH INTO A COLORFUL SPA. SOMETIMES ALL A SMALL SPACE NEEDS IS A BIG SPLASH OF COLOR AND A STRONG DOSE OF FLORALS.

ABOVE TO CREATE A LESS STUDIED LOOK, I MIXED AN ASSORTMENT OF BLOOMING FABRICS ON MY SOFA. WHILE MOST OF THE COLORS IN THE NEEDLEPOINT PILLOW DON'T EXACTLY MATCH THE COLORS IN THE OTHER PATTERNS, THE GROUPING COORDINATES BECAUSE ALL THE PINKS ARE THE SAME.

RIGHT TO GET A BIG IMPACT OUT OF THE PINT-SIZE LIVING-DINING ROOM OF MY OLD CAPE COD COTTAGE, AND TO UNITE ALL ITS DISPARATE ELEMENTS, I COVERED EVERYTHING I COULD IN ROSES. RATHER THAN WALLPAPERING IN A FLORAL, WHICH WOULD HAVE CLOSED UP THE SPACE, I OPTED FOR AIRY WHITE WALLS AND HUNG FLOWER PRINTS AND PLATES INSTEAD.

LEFT IF YOU ARE WORKING WITH A SLIM BUDGET (AS I WAS HERE), THERE'S A WORLD OF GORGEOUS FLORAL SHEETS THAT CAN HELP YOU OUT OF A BIND. HERE I HUNG BEDSHEETS AS WINDOW TREATMENTS, SIMPLY KNOTTING THE FABRIC AT THE CORNERS AND MOUNTING THEM ON HIDDEN NAILS.

ABOVE LIKE AN EARTHY GARDEN BED, THIS GUEST BEDROOM IS A MEDLEY OF FLOWERS. I LOVE THE CRAZY QUILT OF PATTERNS THAT EMERGED WHEN I MIXED AND MATCHED ART, LINENS, AND FRESH FLOWERS WITH THE POSY-COVERED LAMP I FOUND AT A JUNK STORE.

ABOVE USE CLASSIC ELEMENTS SUCH AS WHITE BEDDING, BLACK LAMPSHADES, AND OAK FURNITURE, AND YOUR DESIGN BECOMES TIMELESS.

LEFT BY PAPERING THE WALLS IN A GRID OF TINY FLOWERS AND LEAVES, I MADE THIS ROOM SOFT BUT NOT TOO SWEET. THE PLAID THROW AND CHECKED CARPET ECHO THE DIAMOND MOTIF OF THE FLORAL WALLPAPER AND GROUND THE SPACE IN SENSIBLE GREENS.

LEFT WANT A LOW-COMMITMENT WAY TO SURROUND YOURSELF WITH FLORALS? HANG BED CURTAINS LIKE THESE. AS THE SEASONS CHANGE OR AS YOUR MOOD SWAYS, SIMPLY REPLACE THEM. (CATH KIDSTON, DESIGNER)

OPPOSITE ROSES GROWING ON WOODY VINES SUIT THE RUSTIC SETTING OF THIS HOME. TO ECHO THE PLANTS AND WALLPAPER PATTERN, THE DESIGNER ADDED A FEW ROSE-PATTERN TOSS PILLOWS TO THE ADIRONDACK-STYLE BENCHES. (REBECCA ELLSLEY, DESIGNER)

PAGES 208–209 A BLUE RUG SPREADS BLOSSOMS ACROSS THE FLOOR IN THIS ABUNDANTLY FLORAL ROOM. TO BALANCE THE VISUAL WEIGHT OF THE RUG AND CONTINUE THE FLOWERY THEME, THE WINDOWS, WALLS, OTTOMAN, AND TOSS PILLOWS WEAR A FLORAL WITH SIMILAR COLORS ON A WHITE BACKGROUND. CHECKS, STRIPES, COORDINATING FLORALS, AND SOLID BLOCKS OF COLOR PULL THE YELLOWS, PINKS, AND BLUES FROM THE PRIMARY PATTERN TO COMPLETE THE SCHEME. (TONY BARATTA AND BILL DIAMOND, DESIGNERS)

OPPOSITE SET IN THE SAME HOUSE AS THE LIVING ROOM ON PAGES 208–209, THIS DINING ROOM CONTINUES THE GARDEN THEME. HERE TRELLISLIKE LATTICE CLIMBS THE WALLS, WHILE FLOWERS TAKE OVER THE FLOOR, FURNITURE, DRAPERIES, AND TABLETOP.

(TONY BARATTA AND BILL DIAMOND, DESIGNERS)

ABOVE IF YOU TEAM A ROSE PATTERN WITH SOLID FABRICS THAT REPEAT THE FLORAL'S COLORS, YOU GET A SIMPLER SCHEME. TO PUMP UP THE FLOWER VOLUME JUST A LITTLE, ADD ACCENT PILLOWS WITH A FLORAL MOTIF.

(LOUISE BROOKS, DESIGNER)

{Plaid & Check}

Essentially plaids and checks do the same thing: They are blocks of color that repeat a pattern and color combination over and over, like squares on a chessboard. Plaids have roots in Scotland, where clans were known by the patterns they wore. (To this day certain classic patterns are known by Scottish surnames.) To my mind, plaids can be truly sophisticated, while two-tone checks are generally just plain peppy. No matter their attitude, I tend to incorporate plaids and checks as accents rather than as the primary pattern in a room. Every now and then, though, I make an exception. Checks are wonderful in a kid's room, for instance, and are great on the floors and walls of a kitchen, especially if it has a lot of cabinets. And I have done a plaid-dominated room too, for a Scottish client whose sweet wife let him do his thing in the house. He said that if he had his way, he would upholster the entire world

I DESIGNED THIS WINDOW SEAT FOR A COUPLE, AND THE FABRICS WERE A HIT WITH BOTH HUSBAND AND WIFE. I'VE NOTICED THAT IF I PUT SOME PLAID IN A ROOM—LIKE THAT ON THE CUSHIONS AND TOSS PILLOWS HERE—I CAN GET AWAY WITH ADDING A FEW FEMININE TOUCHES WITHOUT TOO MUCH GRUMBLING FROM THE MAN OF THE HOUSE.

"PEOPLE THINK PLAIDS AND CHECKS ARE BUSY, BUT IT DEPENDS ON THE TONAL CONTRAST. IF THE COLORS ARE EITHER ALL LIGHT OR ALL DARK, YOU GET A VERY SOOTHING PATTERN."

OPPOSITE WOVEN IN CASUAL COTTON FABRIC, THIS CORAL RED CHECK GIVES THE DRAPERIES AN INFORMAL TONE THAT REFLECTS THE COUNTRY SETTING OF THIS HOUSE. I HAD A LOT OF FUN DESIGNING THE HANGING LIGHT; THE BOTTOM FRINGED TRIM IS MADE FROM A PLAID RIBBON AND TASSELS.

RIGHT NOTICE HOW THE PLAID TOSS PILLOWS HERE ARE THE OPPOSITE (MORE WHITE THAN BLUE) OF THE PLAID SEAT CUSHIONS (MORE BLUE THAN WHITE). WORKING IN THE SAME COLORWAY BUT REVERSING HUES IS AN EASY TRICK FOR PAIRING TWO DIFFERENT PLAIDS.

in plaid. We stopped just short of that, with a custom-made rug in a green and blue Hunting MacLeod plaid that ran through the dining room and living room, down the hall, and up the stairs. It worked because although plaid clearly dominated, there were solid blocks of color to offset the busyness of the pattern.

To get such balance when I'm using plaids or checks as an accent rather than as the main attraction, I make sure that if I have a touch of either one on one side of the room, I repeat the same fabric somewhere on the other side. For example, say I put a couple of plump plaid pillows on a plain sofa. Across the room let's imagine there's a little side chair with an upholstered seat. To get the balance, I'll upholster the chair seat with plaid. Scattering the pattern like that creates room rhythm. (CONTINUED ON PAGE 219)

This three-season porch sits just beyond a set of French doors draped in checked window treatments, so I chose complementary checks here for variety in the same pattern family. Placing the larger-scale checks on the floor anchors the room, while floral toss pillows and cushions along with curvy furniture soften the sharp edges of the dominant pattern.

"I CAN'T THINK OF A DEPRESSING CHECK—IT'S JUST A HAPPY PATTERN."

OPPOSITE OUTDOOR FABRICS ARE MORE VARIED THAN EVER, WITH MANY PATTERNS AND COLORS AVAILABLE IN FADE-PROOF, MOISTURE-RESISTANT SYNTHETICS THAT HAVE THE SAME FEEL AS INTERIOR FABRICS. HERE CHECKS AND MY FAVORITE MOTIF, FLORALS, COMBINE IN A PATTERN I CHOSE BECAUSE IT NEATLY ECHOES THE LATTICE GRID ON THE FENCE.

RIGHT PLAID AND CHECK PATTERNS EASILY BLEND WITH OTHER PATTERNS, SOMETIMES EVEN IN THE SAME PRINT. THE TABLECLOTH HERE INCORPORATES FLOWERS INTO A GRID. NOTICE HOW THE COLORFUL LINES FRAME THE BLOOMS.

Plaids and checks work well as accents in any room because they look just as great with any other print or pattern as they do with solids. It is fairly easy to combine them with seemingly complex patterns like toiles and florals. In such cases color is key, but so is scale. As for the latter, focus on what's headlining. If the primary fabric is a floral with large flowers, for instance, I use a small-scale plaid to offset it. If the primary print is a smaller floral with little springy blooms, I go for either a large or small plaid. If I'm using toile as the primary print, I really like teaming it up with a check, because both are two-tone patterns and thus they work beautifully together. In each case notice how the patterns contrast: The soft, round lines of a toile or floral are the complete opposite of the straight lines of a check or plaid.

ABOVE THE NATURAL BUSYNESS OF PLAIDS AND CHECKS CAN BE TONED DOWN WITH SOFT, NEUTRAL COLORS. HERE THE NATURAL-WOOD-AND-WHITE CHECK FLOOR PATTERN IS BOLDER THAN ANY OF THE FABRICS, SO IT HELPS GROUND THE MONOCHROMATIC COLOR SCHEME. VARIETY IN THE SCALE OF THE PLAIDS AT THE WINDOW AND ON THE DESK CHAIR KEEPS THE MIX INTERESTING.

(KATHRYNE DAHLMAN AND CAREN COLBURN, DESIGNERS)

RIGHT SILK HAS AN IRIDESCENCE THAT INFUSES A PATTERN WITH LUSTROUS GLAMOUR. HERE SILK TAFFETA DRAPERIES AND A NEIGHBORING SILK SLIPCOVERED DESK CHAIR BRING TWO PLAIDS INTO THE MIX. I'M ALWAYS AMAZED HOW SOMETHING AS POTENTIALLY RUGGED AS A PLAID CAN BE DOMESTICATED BY SUCH A REFINED MATERIAL.

(KATHRYNE DAHLMAN AND CAREN COLBURN, DESIGNERS)

LEFT PAIR PLAID WITH STRIPES AND YOU GET A WONDERFUL PLAY OF PATTERNS. DRAW THE DRAPERIES IN THIS DINING ROOM, AND THE HORIZONTAL LINES CONTRAST WITH THE VERTICAL WALLPAPER FOR A HANDSOME DANCE OF NEUTRAL-COLOR PATTERNS. THE DESIGNER LINKED THE PLAID PATTERN TO THE WINDOW HARDWARE BY PAINTING THE RODS AND RINGS IN TWO DIFFERENT COLORS INSPIRED BY THE CLOTH. (MARK PHELPS, DESIGNER)

RIGHT CHECKS AND PLAIDS CREATE A SOFT HAVEN THANKS TO THE MUTED TONES OF EACH PATTERN. BOXY PATTERNS SHOW UP IN THE FURNISHINGS TOO— IN THE OVERALL SHAPE OF THE BED, ITS CANOPY LINES, AND ITS MOLDING. (TISH KEY, DESIGNER)

LEFT ELEGANT PLAID DRAPERIES HARMONIZE WITH THE CARAMEL-COLOR WALLS OF THIS GENTLEMAN'S DRESSING ROOM. NOTICE HOW HANGING IDENTICALLY FRAMED 19TH-CENTURY FASHION-PLATE ETCHINGS FROM FLOOR TO CEILING AND ABOVE THE WINDOWS CREATES AN ADDITIONAL GEOMETRIC PATTERN TO COMPLEMENT THE PLAID. (FRED ROOT AND ANTHONY FEO, DESIGNERS)

OPPOSITE THE RICH COLORS OF THE GOLDEN PINE MOLDING, DARK GREEN WALLS, AND RED SIDE CHAIR ARE CAPTURED IN THE PLAID VALANCES THAT CAP THE WINDOWS. WITH WOODWORK THIS HANDSOME, DRAPERY PANELS ARE UNNECESSARY. (FRED ROOT AND ANTHONY FEO, DESIGNERS)

LEFT WHILE THIS ROOM IS DOMINATED BY A SOUND MARRIAGE OF PLAIDS AND CHECKS, ADDING A PAIR OF FLORAL CHAIRS AND A GRID-PATTERN RUG THAT'S PUNCTUATED WITH SMALL FLOWERS GIVES THE SETTING DEPTH WITH A SOFT UNDERTONE.

(CHARLES FAUDREE, DESIGNER)

ABOVE WRAPPING A ROOM IN CHECKS IS NOT FOR THE FAINT OF HEART. BECAUSE THE BOUQUETS ON THE MOSTLY YELLOW CHAIRS FEATURE THE SAME VIBRANT SHADE OF RED AS THE WALLS, THE TWO PATTERNS FORM A SUCCESSFUL COLLAGE.

(NANCY SERAFINI, DESIGNER)

RIGHT HERE'S HOW TO CELEBRATE PLAID—PINK PLAID, NO LESS—TO THE HILT. TO GIVE THE LOUNGE SOME VISUAL BALANCE, THE DESIGNERS USED THE ACCENT HUE OF BLUE AS A COUNTERPOINT TO THE PINK. FOR A MORE LOW-KEY LOOK, THEY COULD HAVE OPTED FOR CLOUD WHITE AS THE SOLE DETAILING COLOR, BUT WHERE'S THE FUN THERE?
(TONY BARATTA AND BILL DIAMOND, DESIGNERS)

PAGES 230–231
CONSIDER THE FLOOR THE FIFTH WALL IN ANY SPACE, AND YOU'LL WANT TO DRESS IT. THE DESIGNER CHOSE A PLAID RUG WITH A SUBTLE NEUTRAL PALETTE AND BUILT THE ROOM AROUND IT. COLORS FROM THE PATTERN APPEAR AS SOLIDS ON THE WALLS, WINDOWS, BED SKIRT, FIREPLACE, AND FURNISHINGS.
(JOHN DE BASTIANI, DESIGNER)

OPPOSITE THIS ROOM IS A CANVAS FOR TWO THINGS: THE TOSS PILLOWS AND THE TURQUOISE FIGURES THAT REPEAT THE BLUE OF THE PLAID PATTERN. THIS ROOM AND THE ONE AT RIGHT SHOW HOW A LITTLE PATTERN CAN PACK A POWERFUL PUNCH.

(MIMI REILLY, DESIGNER)

RIGHT EVEN A LITTLE PLAID GIVES A ROOM ADDED CHARACTER. A SINGLE ACCENT WALL COVERED IN A RAINBOW PLAID MAKES A STRIKING FOCAL POINT THAT ALSO SETS THE COLOR PALETTE. WHILE PLAIDS ARE TYPICALLY THOUGHT OF AS A TRADITIONAL PATTERN, THIS OFFICE SMACKS OF CONTEMPORARY POP STYLE.

(ANDREW FLESHER, DESIGNER)

{Stripes

Stripes are a simple, humble pattern, and that makes them perfect for decorating pros and novices alike to play with. I love using them on pillows, draperies, and as upholstery, and I love covering walls with them. I use them everywhere, in any space, because there's so much that you can get a stripe to do.

Before you get stripe-happy, consider what mood you hope to achieve by filling your space with color and pattern. Because stripes are so graphic, the tonal contrast will dictate the feeling the pattern creates. For instance, if you choose bright red and white, it's going to feel joyous and active. If you choose beige and white, it's going to feel sedate and sophisticated. If you choose a ticking—thin, dark stripes, typically blue on an off-white cotton twill—it's going to feel gentle and casual.

Once you know what colors and what tones you'll use, you can get down to decorating. With draperies, I often let the stripes run down the height of a window and then I add a

SOMETIMES DESIGNERS INHERIT ELEMENTS THEY HAVE TO WORK AROUND, BUT HERE I SCORED A GOLD MINE: DEMURELY STRIPED WALLPAPER IN A WONDERFUL NEUTRAL TONE. TO ADD DEPTH TO THE ROOM, I LAYERED ON FLORALS AND PLAIDS IN THE SAME ELEGANT HUES AS THE DOMINANT PATTERN.

"IF YOU WANT A WONDERFUL ROOM FILLED WITH PATTERN, BUT YOU'RE UNSURE HOW TO GET THERE, STICK WITH STRIPES AND YOU CAN'T GO WRONG."

OPPOSITE BOYS SEEM
TO GO FOR STRIPES, AND
THAT WAS THE CASE IN
THIS YOUNG MAN'S ROOM.
WHILE THE NEUTRAL
WALL ACCENTUATES THE
HEADBOARD, THE BED
LINENS ADD COLOR AND
A NONLINEAR PATTERN,
MAKING THE ROOM FEEL
HOMEY.

RIGHT HANG FRAMED
PIECES ON A STRIPED
BACKGROUND AND YOU
CAN ALWAYS KEEP THEM
STRAIGHT—JUST LINE UP
THE FRAMES WITH THE
PATTERN ON THE WALL.
AS FOR THE ARTWORK? I
CHOSE HUNTING SCENES
AND FIGURINES TO
COMPLEMENT THE BLUE
AND YELLOW TOILE BED
LINENS, WHICH FEATURE
MAN'S BEST FRIEND
(OPPOSITE).

2-inch-wide diagonal stripe border along the leading edges and along the bottom. This outlines the draperies and gives them a frame. I do that a lot, using graphic patterns such as checks, plaids, and stripes for framing other softer patterns. Take a toss pillow, for example. Cut a piece of striped fabric on the diagonal and you have a wonderful contrast welting.

Turning a stripe on its head like that is guaranteed fun. I've done it with a room that I covered in ticking—the stripes met in triangular pieces at the center of the ceiling, and you got the feeling you were in a tent (see page 53). To get the same effect without a big commitment, try this: Cut four equal triangles out of a striped fabric and piece them back together so that the stripes outline the outside of a pillow, making a

box shape. Or take the same four triangles and piece them together in the opposite way to make a cross. Manipulating the fabric in that way creates a strong new pattern, one that works well with curvy prints, such as florals. Because stripes get along with so many other patterns, it's popular to use them with as many as five other prints to upholster a single piece of furniture for a cottage look. Sounds good to me—you can never get enough of a good thing, right?

ABOVE I USED A MILLION DIFFERENT FABRICS IN THIS SPACE (I'M HARDLY EXAGGERATING), AND THE GREEN STRIPED WINDOW TREATMENTS HELP TO CREATE A LITTLE ORDER IN THE FRENZY. WHEN STRIPES ARE USED AS DRAPERIES, THEY APPEAR TO ELONGATE THE PANELS AND GIVE THE ILLUSION OF HIGHER CEILINGS.

OPPOSITE MULTICOLOR STRIPES ARE MARVELOUS FOR GENERATING A COMPLETE COLOR SCHEME FOR ANY SETTING. THE BLUE, GREEN, AND YELLOW OF THESE GAZEBO HANGINGS MADE ROCKING CHAIR CUSHIONS IN THE SAME PALETTE AN OBVIOUS CHOICE.

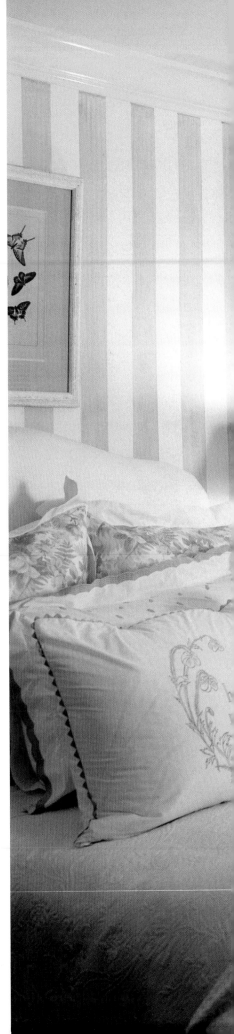

LEFT AND RIGHT
THE DIFFERENT COLOR INTENSITY OF THE GREEN STRIPES IN EACH OF THESE ROOMS CREATES TWO COMPLETELY DIFFERENT MOODS AND ENVIRONMENTS. THE ONE AT RIGHT FEELS PUNCHY AND FULL OF ENERGY AND IS PERFECT FOR A WEEKEND GUEST'S STAY. THE ONE AT LEFT, HOWEVER, IS A RESTFUL ENVIRONMENT THAT'S WELL-SUITED FOR A MASTER SUITE. NOTE THAT THE MIRROR AT LEFT LEANS TOWARD SILVER TONES, WHILE THE ONE IN THE APPLE GREEN ROOM WEARS A GILDED FRAME, UNDERSCORING THE COOL VERSUS WARM TONES IN THE GREENS.
(LEFT: STEPHANIE STOKES, DESIGNER)
(OPPOSITE: DIANE CHAPMAN, DESIGNER)

LEFT AT FIRST GLANCE IT'S EASY TO OVERLOOK THIS WALLPAPER BECAUSE IT SEEMS SO SIMPLE. BUT THE TWO-TONE STRIPE, HIGHLIGHTED WITH A GOLD PINSTRIPE, IS A QUIETLY SOPHISTICATED PATTERN THAT MAKES AN ELEGANT BACKGROUND FOR FLORAL FABRICS AND ANTIQUE PORCELAINS.
(SCOTT SALVATOR AND MICHAEL ZABRISKIE, DESIGNERS)

ABOVE MULTICOLOR STRIPES GIVE YOU OPTIONS FOR COLOR SCHEMES. HERE THE BLUE STRIPE IN THE WALLPAPER IS WIDER AND MORE PRONOUNCED, BUT PULLING OUT THE LIME HUE FOR THE SLIPCOVERS PUSHES THE ROOM'S COLOR MOOD TO THE WARMER SIDE OF THE COLOR WHEEL.
(MATTHEW PATRICK SMYTH, DESIGNER)

LEFT STRIPES LAID OUT HORIZONTALLY CAN MAKE A ROOM SEEM WIDER THAN IT IS. HORIZONTAL STRIPES MAKE THIS BATH APPEAR OPEN AND SPACIOUS. THE THICK BANDS OF NEUTRAL COLORS EXAGGERATE THE EFFECT.

(SUSAN FERRIS, DESIGNER)

OPPOSITE WHAT A TERRIFIC IDEA IT WAS TO PAINT THESE CEILING BEAMS BLUE TO MIMIC THE BLUE STRIPE OF THE RUG AND FABRICS. THIS ROOM IS A GOOD REMINDER TO LOOK AROUND ANY SPACE FOR EXISTING, INHERENT PATTERNS AND DRAW THEM INTO YOUR MIX OF FABRIC AND WALLPAPER PATTERNS.

(THOMAS BARTLETT, DESIGNER)

LEFT MAYBE IT'S HAPPY CHANCE, BUT THE RED, WHITE, AND BLUE STRIPES ON THE LIVING ROOM FABRICS SEEM TO REPLICATE THE VERTICAL LINES OF THE BEADED-BOARD SHELVING AND DOOR. THE WALL ART IN THE ADJOINING ROOM ALSO PICKS UP THE BLUE IN THE FABRIC STRIPE, A NEAT WAY OF TYING THE TWO ROOMS TOGETHER.

(ELIZABETH MORASH AND JON HATTAWAY, DESIGNERS)

ABOVE I TEND TO USE LOTS OF DIFFERENT PRINTS IN ANY GIVEN SPACE, BUT THIS NEARLY SINGLE-PATTERN LOOK WORKS BRILLIANTLY. THE COFFEE TABLE OTTOMAN PROVIDES ENOUGH CONTRAST TO KEEP THE LINES FROM BECOMING OVERWHELMING, AND THE SOLID WHITE WALLS AND SOLID-COLOR FLOOR FURTHER BALANCE THE LOOK.

(ELIZABETH MORASH AND JON HATTAWAY, DESIGNERS)

OPPOSITE THE IDEA OF CHOOSING SMALL, MEDIUM, AND LARGE PRINTS APPLIES TO STRIPES TOO. LOOK AT THE RANGE IN THIS ROOM, FROM TINY PINSTRIPES IN THE ROMAN SHADES TO WIDE BANDS OF BLUE AND WHITE ON THE SETTEE. CHECKS, FLORALS, AND SOLIDS ADD COTTAGE-STYLE VARIETY, BUT IT'S THE STRIPES THAT SET THE TONE.

(LYNN VON KERSTING, DESIGNER)

RIGHT THOUGH THERE ARE SEVERAL PATTERNS IN THIS ROOM—FROM THE HAND-STENCILED LINEN DIRECTOIRE WALLCOVERING TO THE PLAID SIDE CHAIR AND THE TEXTURED RUG— IT'S THE STRIPES THAT DOMINATE THE SPACE. THE HIGH CONTRAST OF THEIR WHITE AND GRAY BANDS PUMPS UP THE IMPACT.

(SUZI BRIGGS, DESIGNER)

ABOVE USING STRIPED WALLPAPER IN TWO RICH TONES CAN GIVE YOU AN EFFECT SIMILAR TO THAT OF A SOLID-COLOR WALL, WITH NONE OF THE STERILITY OF THE LATTER. HERE A SIMPLE PATTERN OF CORAL AND RED DELIVERS A REFINED LOOK.

(JOE MCKINNON, DESIGNER)

RIGHT TWO STRIPED CHAIRS TONE DOWN THE ACTION IN A SPACE DOMINATED BY MORE-COMPLEX PATTERNS ON THE RUG, WALLS, MANTEL, AND FIREPLACE.

(MARSHALL WATSON, DESIGNER)

{Found Pattern

Before you cut your first fabric sample or buy a single piece of furniture, look for patterns in the architectural details of a room. These found patterns span the walls, ceilings, and floors and include decorative molding and trim, chair rails and wainscoting, recessed wall paneling and beaded board, pressed-tin ceilings, exposed beams, stair rails, cabinetry, built-in shelves, and more.

Step back and take a look. If pattern as I define it is shape on shape and shape on backgrounds, what existing shapes are in the room you're working on? What are the existing backgrounds? And what are the existing textures? (These textures often come from the materials used: a basket weave of porous bricks on the floor, stripes of exposed beams overhead, a mosaic of glossy tiles around the bath, or a crazy quilt of rough stones around a fireplace.) Every element in a space has its own built-in pattern, and you can play it up or down with color.

If you're more comfortable in a subtle, quiet room, then paint these wonderful existing patterns all white or the same color. Call out the details in a bold color, however, to save a ho-hum room from a bland fate. I'm a fan of all-white

I USED A CIRCLE MOTIF (REMINISCENT OF A SHIP CAPTAIN'S WHEEL) THROUGHOUT THIS HOUSE AND DESIGNED THE STAIR RAILS TO REPEAT THE SHAPE. WORKING A PATTERN INTO THE STRUCTURE MAKES IT PART OF THE IDENTITY OF THE PLACE.

{ "ADD ARCHITECTURAL DETAILS TO AN OTHERWISE BLAND ROOM, AND SUDDENLY THE SPACE IS FILLED WITH PATTERNS AND TEXTURES."

OPPOSITE HIGH HUMIDITY MADE VENTILATION A NECESSITY IN THE CABINETS AT MY LAST BEACH COTTAGE. TO LET THE DOORS BREATHE IN STYLE, I HAD SLOTS AND HOLES CUT INTO THE WOOD IN AN ARTS AND CRAFTS-INSPIRED PATTERN.

RIGHT THIS IS THE MANTEL FROM THE HOUSE ON PAGE 253. I HAD A CARPENTER CARVE THE SHAPES IN THE RAILING INTO THE MANTEL. CUSTOM WOODWORK IS PRICEY BUT PRICELESS FOR A COHESIVE, PERSONALIZED PATTERN.

cabinetry and all-white trim. All-white makes it easy to change out the other colors in a room, and it always looks nice and fresh. But if you like a lot going on in a room, opt for contrast. Accentuate the found patterns by pairing them with a different background color pulled from the overall color scheme.

If you're starting with a blank slate of drywall and minimal or no trim, have fun and design your own details. I've done houses where the details are themed—from railings and moldings to the window and door headers. I've also added 1×4-inch flat molding around doors and windows and as a baseboard for a great farmhouse look. On the more formal side, crown molding can dress up a room if its ceilings are 8 feet or higher; if the ceiling is lower than that, it's best to deemphasize it. If a room can handle crown molding, get a friend to hold sample trim in place and see which size looks best. Generally, the higher the ceiling, the larger and more elaborate the molding.

To add texture and pattern to a bare wall, why not create your own paneled look? First nail a 1×4-inch chair rail around the room, about two-thirds up the wall from the floor. Nail a 1×5-inch baseboard along the base of the walls. Then use strips of 2×½-inch lattice to create large, evenly spaced rectangles or squares between the chair rail and the baseboard. Paint the woodwork and the walls inside the faux panels with the same semigloss or gloss paint, and wallpaper above the chair rail. It's inexpensive and creates an old-fashioned recessed-panel pattern.

Found patterns come in the form of collections too, and I'm a big collector. I have collections of antique ceramic sardine boxes; needlepoint pillows; vases (yellow vases, white vases, and blue vases); and 1950s paint-by-numbers tropical birds I've been buying online—don't even get me started on those! The great thing about these objects is that they give me a strong sense of being at home. Every single piece is there because I chose it and placed it somewhere special. My "stuff" surrounds me with personality and adds visual play to my rooms.

LEFT | WORKED WITH AN ARCHITECT TO LIFT THE ROOF OF THIS STAIRWELL AND ADD WHAT APPEARS TO BE 360 DEGREES OF WINDOWS AND GRIDS IN TOWER FORM. THE WRAPAROUND EFFECT IS AN ILLUSION, THOUGH: THREE SIDES OF THE SPACE ARE MERELY MIRRORED GLASS REFLECTING THE ONE TRUE WINDOW. AS YOU CAN SEE BY THE LIGHT FIXTURE, THE SKY IS A PAINTED ILLUSION.

OPPOSITE | FOUND THE BLUE AND YELLOW STAINED-GLASS WINDOW IN A LOCAL SALVAGE YARD AND SET IT BELOW THE SKYLIGHT. NOW ITS PATTERN AND COLORS PLAY IN THE BRIGHT ROOM ON SUNNY DAYS.

{ "INCORPORATE BUILT-IN FEATURES AND YOU CAN BOOST THE COLOR, PATTERN, AND TEXTURE IN A SPACE."

OPPOSITE PATTERNS CAN BE MADE BY HANGING OBJECTS ON THE WALL OR, AS IN THIS ROOM, FROM THE CEILING. I LOVE THE WAY THE DELICATE GLASS OF THE WINE GOBLETS INTERACTS WITH THE ROUGH-HEWN TIMBERS.
(MARK WILKINSON, DESIGNER)

ABOVE WHEN YOU LOOK AT A CEILING AS AN EXPANSIVE CANVAS, ADDING PATTERN BECOMES IRRESISTIBLE. HERE I INCORPORATED A PRESSED-TIN FACADE TO REPEAT THE SHIP'S WHEEL THEME THAT APPEARS THROUGHOUT THE HOUSE.

LEFT ONE OF MY FAVORITE WAYS TO BRING PATTERN TO A PLAIN CEILING IS TO COVER IT WITH BEADED-BOARD PLANKS. THE DESIGNER TRIMMED THE PERIMETER OF THE VAULTED CEILING WITH NAUTICAL-INSPIRED ROPE MOLDING AND USED SMALL BRACKETS TO ACCENTUATE THE VAULT.
(STUART DISSTON, ARCHITECT)

RIGHT IN THE PAST PLASTER CASTS FORMED CLASSIC CEILING DETAILS. POLYURETHANE APPLIQUÉS ARE NOW USED IN THE SAME WAY. NO MATTER THE MEDIUM, STATELY PATTERNS LIKE THIS MEDALLION-FILLED HONEYCOMB MAKE ANY HIGH CEILING MORE DRAMATIC.
(BARRY DIXON, DESIGNER)

"IF YOU ASK ME, A BARE
WALL JUST BEGS FOR
EMBELLISHMENT."

264

LEFT THE GRID FORMED BY THESE TRELLISES LOOKS ALMOST LIKE A NATURAL PLAID MADE OF CEDAR. MORE THAN MERELY DECORATIVE, IT GAVE ME A PLACE TO HANG THE BARBECUE UTENSILS AT MY FORMER BEACH HOUSE.

ABOVE LOG WALLS GIVE TEXTURE AND PATTERN TO ANY SPACE, INSIDE OR OUT. THIS IS THE SCREEN PORCH OF MY ONE-TIME LAKE CABIN, AND THE WALLS INFLUENCED THE WAY I DECORATED THE ENTIRE HOME.

LEFT AS THE SEASONS PASS, THIS WONDERFUL WALLSCAPE PATTERN WILL EVOLVE, CHANGING AS THE STOCKPILE OF LOGS IS DIMINISHED AND REPLENISHED. SOMETIMES THE SIMPLEST MATERIALS ADD THE MOST INTEREST TO YOUR ENVIRONMENT.

(SANDY GALLIN, DESIGNER, FIREWOOD RACK; SCOTT MITCHELL, ARCHITECT)

RIGHT TILE BACKSPLASHES ARE GREAT SPOTS TO WORK IN FOUND PATTERNS, WHETHER THEY ARE MONOCHROMATIC RELIEF IMAGES OR ACTUAL HANDPAINTED SCENES LIKE THIS CUSTOM-DESIGNED PICTORIAL TILE.

LEFT I WANTED THE FLOOR TO REPEAT THE STACKED STONE WALL OF THIS ROOM (NOT VISIBLE FROM THIS ANGLE), SO I DREW ROCKLIKE SHAPES ONTO THE FLOOR WITH CHALK AND HAD A DECORATIVE PAINTER CREATE A FAUX-STONE LOOK.

OPPOSITE THE DOMINANT SOURCE OF COLOR IN THIS KITCHEN COMES FROM THE BISTRO-STYLE TILE DESIGN I MAPPED OUT FOR A CLIENT. FLOOR PATTERNS LIKE THIS ARE ESPECIALLY PRACTICAL IN KITCHENS BECAUSE THEY CAMOUFLAGE SPILLS AND MESSES.

"WHEN YOU HAVE A LOT OF PLAIN SPACE IN A KITCHEN, DO EITHER TILE OR A PAINTED FLOOR TO ADD PATTERN."

LEFT AND ABOVE THE
DECOR OF THESE ROOMS
SEEMS TO SPROUT
FROM THE GROUND UP.
FROM THE SIMPLICITY
OF CHECKERBOARD
(LEFT) TO THE MORE
INTRICATE PAINTED
OCTAGONAL PATTERN
(ABOVE), FLOORS CAN
ADD COLORFUL ACTION
TO ANY SPACE. ON THE
PRACTICAL SIDE, HARD-
WEARING FLOOR PAINT
IS AN INEXPENSIVE
SOLUTION FOR WORN OR
DAMAGED FLOORS.
(LEFT: CHRISTINA DUTTON, DESIGNER))
(ABOVE: GARY MCBOURNIE,
DESIGNER)

LEFT A GANG OF BOTANICAL PRINTS AGAINST A PLAIN WHITE WALL CREATES A RHYTHM OF POSITIVE AND NEGATIVE SHAPES THAT MAKES A LATTICED GRID IN A CORNER OF THIS GUESTHOUSE.

RIGHT TO OFFSET THE STRAIGHT LINES OF THE BANISTER RAILING, I HUNG A SERIES OF PLATES IN A UNIFORM ROW. NOTICE HOW THE FRAMED PRINTS AND PLATES SET ON BRACKETS ON THE WALL BELOW REPEAT THE PAIRING OF CIRCLES AND SQUARES.

"GROUPINGS OF ART AND COLLECTIBLES CREATE PATTERN TOO. THE MORE SPECIFIC THE COLLECTION, THE MORE FUN THE HUNT."

ABOVE THIS WINDOWSILL CRIED OUT FOR DECORATION, SO I ADDED A GROUPING OF CRYSTAL AND GLASS FINIALS MOUNTED ON MARBLE BASES. ALMOST ANY SURFACE CAN BECOME A DISPLAY SHELF LIKE THIS.

OPPOSITE I GATHERED EVERY PRETTY BROKEN AND CHIPPED OLD VASE I HAD AND MIXED THEM IN WITH OTHER COLLECTIBLES TO CREATE A CHORUS OF COLORS AND SHAPES ON THIS POTTING BENCH. SHELVES LIKE THESE ARE IDEAL SPOTS TO PLAY WITH PATTERNS.

OPPOSITE WHEN YOU
MAT, FRAME, AND HANG A
SET OF BLACK AND WHITE
PHOTOS IN UNIFORM
FASHION, IT RESULTS IN
A DELIGHTFUL, ORDERLY
QUILT OF IMAGES. THE
NEAT EFFECT IS ACHIEVED
BY ALIGNING THE EDGES
OF THE FRAMES AT THE
TOP AND BOTTOM OF THE
DISPLAY AND ALLOWING
FOR SLIGHT VARIATIONS
INSIDE THE OVERALL
RECTANGLE.

(SUE BALMFORTH, DESIGNER)

RIGHT I LOVE THE WAY
THE BLACK LINES IN THE
COLLAGES HUNG ON THE
WALL MIMIC THE CURTAIN
RODS. THE YELLOW
BORDERS MATCH THE
YELLOW DRAPERIES. IT'S
ALMOST AS IF THE ROW OF
ARTWORK INSPIRED THE
WINDOW TREATMENTS.

(RITVA HEINO, DESIGNER)

PAGES 278–279
SOMETIMES YOU ONLY
NEED ONE LARGE
PATTERN TO TAKE A
ROOM FROM HO-HUM TO
SPECTACULAR. A WALL
HANGING DOES THE
HONORS IN THIS DINING
SPOT. THE COLLECTION
OF BLUE AND WHITE
POTTERY ON THE BUFFET
CONTINUES THE THEME
HANDSOMELY.

(THOMAS BARTLETT, DESIGNER)

OPPOSITE THE PATTERNS HERE BEGIN WITH THE DISTANT OUTDOOR BRICK WALK AND CONTINUE PAST THE THRESHOLD. A MARBLEIZED WOODEN FLOOR MAKES A SMOOTH TRANSITION BETWEEN THE RUDDY COLORS OUTSIDE AND THE DARK-STAINED STAIR RAIL.

RIGHT IN A STROKE OF GENIUS, THE DESIGNER RELIED ON NATURE'S INTRINSIC PATTERNS—AND COLORS—TO WARM UP AN EXTREMELY PRACTICAL AND HARDY FLOOR. SANDED SMOOTH, SET IN CONCRETE, AND FINISHED WITH POLISH, THE LOG SECTIONS SEEM TO FLOAT LIKE LILY PADS IN A POND. WHEN YOU HAVE A BUILT-IN PATTERN LIKE THIS, SHOW IT OFF BY BUILDING YOUR ROOM AROUND IT.

(RICHARD OLSEN, ARCHITECT)

GLOSSARY

ADIRONDACK: Rustic style typically achieved with natural materials that originated in the Northeast's Adirondack mountain range in the 1880s. Examples include log cabins, rough-hewn sculptures, and tree-limb or twig chairs and railings.

AMERICANA: Decorative accessories and furniture with a handcrafted, simple appearance reminiscent of early American interiors. Examples include quilts, wooden hutches, and Windsor chairs. Cultural icons such as eagles and simple patterns such as gingham are often incorporated.

ARCHITECTURAL DETAILS: The built-in aspects of a room that give character to its overall structure. Can be a built-in bookshelf, stair railing, window, molding, paneling, pressed-tin ceiling, and more.

ARTS AND CRAFTS: A style popular in America during the late 1800s and early 1900s. Originating in Great Britain, the Arts and Crafts movement was a philosophical and aesthetic reaction to industrialization and mass production. It celebrated handcrafted artisanship, traditional techniques, and "honesty" in the use of materials. In furniture the look is characterized by natural finishes and spare adornments. One of the best-known American designers in the Arts and Crafts style was Gustav Stickley, whose straight-lined oak furniture was called Mission style.

AUBUSSON: Woven wool rug originally from Persia. First came to France (and from there to the rest of western Europe) in the 1600s. Typically features romantic floral patterns.

BACKSPLASH: In a kitchen or bath, the wall behind a basin that typically gets wet or soiled from use. Usually made of tile or some other easy-to-clean surface.

BALUSTRADE: A railing supported by posts.

BASEBOARD: Decorative trim that dresses the seam between a floor and wall.

BATTING: Flat padding generally used to fill quilts and upholster some furniture.

BEADED BOARD: Wood paneling with parallel routed grooves. Sometimes used under chair rails as wainscoting or to cover ceilings and entire walls for a cottage look.

BIEDERMEIER: German and Austrian furniture style from the early to mid 1800s. Generally made of light-color woods with less ornate silhouettes than the heavily embellished Empire pieces of the same time.

BOLSTER: A cylindrical decorative pillow, sometimes called a neck roll.

BOLT: In decorating terms, fabric yardage wrapped around a cardboard tube or panel and hung or posted on display racks in a fabric shop.

BRACKET: A brace that holds up a shelf or roof. Decorative brackets are also called corbels.

CABANA: An outdoor shelter, sometimes with fabric walls, often found at the beach.

CANTONESE CHINA: A type of porcelain made in Canton, China, for export to Europe in the 18th and early 19th centuries. Typically blue scenes on white backgrounds.

CHAIR RAIL: Trim or molding affixed to the walls of a room at a uniform height, where the top of a chair would meet a wall. Originally meant to protect walls from being damaged or nicked by chairs, but often used solely for decorative purposes.

CHAISE: A chair with an elongated seat that allows one to recline as on a sofa.

CHECK: A pattern of same-size squares in alternating colors. Akin to plaid.

CHINOISERIE: Furniture and accessories decorated with Asiatic scenes or Chinese motifs. Pieces are often lacquered.

CHINTZ: Cotton material finished with a glaze that gives it a high sheen.

COLOR FAMILY: Colors that relate to one another. For example, all hues, tints, tones, and shades of blue are in the blue color family. Likewise, all green-blues are similarly related.

COLORWAY: The dominant color in the palette of hues used in a print, whether on fabric or on a wallcovering.

COLOR WHEEL: A graphic decorating and art tool that arranges colors in a circle, with related colors appearing side by side as pie pieces.

COMPLEMENTARY COLORS: Colors that sit directly across from one another on the color wheel.

CONTRAST: Opposing shapes, colors, and elements that, when placed near one another, amplify the intensity of their differences. For example, black and white are highly contrasting colors, and circles and squares are highly contrasting shapes.

COOL COLORS: Colors with blue and gray undertones that create a cool impression and feeling. Can make a space feel expansive and airy.

DAMASK: A weighty upholstery fabric of linen, cotton, silk, or synthetic fibers woven in such a way that a flat satin-weave pattern contrasts with the plain-weave background.

DELFT TILES: White tiles with handpainted, glazed blue patterns and simple scenes. Style first popularized in Holland during the 1500s.

DIRECTOIRE: French decorating style of the late 1700s that bridged the Louis XIV and Empire periods. Is characterized by less-elaborate silhouettes and an affinity for classic Greco-Roman elements.

DOMINANT COLOR: On a piece of fabric, in a pattern, or throughout a room, the color that most commands your attention.

DOMINANT FABRIC: The fabric that inspires a room's color palette and its style. Dictates the mix of other fabrics used in the space.

DUVET COVER: A bed comforter cover.

FAUX: French term meaning fake or an imitation.

FLOOR PLAN: The map of a room or space. Includes boundary walls, built-in elements, and furniture.

FLORAL: A print with patterns of a flower or flowers.

FRENCH COUNTRY: A casually elegant style of decorating that mimics rural homes in France. Rustic elements—plaster walls, worn wooden floors, stone fireplaces—mingle with refined patterns such as toile printed on cotton. Color palettes range from blue and yellow to ocher and pink.

GIMP: Small, flat woven tape traditionally used to cover staples and tacks in upholstered furniture.

HALF-TESTER: A partial canopy that only covers a portion of a bed and is usually affixed to the wall over a headboard.

HEADER: Horizontal piece of wood or trim over the top of a window or door.

HOLDBACKS: Hooks, knobs, or other devices used to keep drapery panels drawn back from the window.

HUE: The gradation of a color. May also refer to the purest grade of a color. For example: true blue, true red, true yellow.

LATTICE: A grid pattern that can be made of wood and used as a trellis, or one that is simulated on a print.

LEAD EDGE: The side of one drapery panel that meets its partner panel at the middle of a window covering.

LOGGIA: A room or entrance porch within the body of a house that is open to the outdoors on at least one side.

MANTEL: A shelf that usually sits over a fireplace but can be mounted elsewhere too.

MARBLEIZED: A surface painted to mimic the look of marble.

MERCURY GLASS: Glass that's been blown to encase a silver solution, which gives the object a mirrored look. Was first fashionable from the late 1800s up through the 1930s and has seen a recent resurgence in popularity.

MOLDING: Decorative trim that outlines and otherwise embellishes walls and other architectural elements. Sometimes used to refer to trim on furniture as well.

MONOCHROMATIC: A color palette created from the same color family or color hue.

MOTIF: A recurring theme, pattern, or element in a design.

MURANO GLASS: Glass pieces that typify a style of glassmaking first made famous in the 13th century on one of the five Venetian islands collectively known as Murano. Highly ornamental, Murano glass often features cut patterns and elaborate silhouettes.

NEUTRAL: Colors that have been dulled down in value by adding gray or brown.

PAISLEY: A swirled, colorful print bearing a teardrop or leaf motif. Has roots in Persia, India, and Scotland.

PALETTE: The group of colors used in a particular setting, on a pattern, or in a print.

PANELING: A piece of wood that creates a rectangular (or square) pattern. Can have a recessed or protruding contour. Is often outlined with trim and seen as wainscoting on walls or as embellishments on furniture.

PARQUET: Interlocking pieces of wood that form a distinct pattern on a surface, usually a floor.

PATTERN: A design in which elements are repeated to create visual interest. Can refer to a print or an interplay of shapes.

PLAID: A pattern of checks. Tartan plaids are now synonymous with what's commonly called a plaid, which refers to a pattern with three or more bands of colors woven into a grid. Has roots in Scotland and northern England.

PRESSED TIN: Tin tiles and panels embossed or impressed with a pattern and used to cover ceilings for decorative purposes. Sometimes used to recall the look of plaster medallions and moldings, other times used to cover an unattractive or dull surface.

PRIMARY COLOR: One of the founding colors in the color wheel: red, yellow, and blue. All other colors are blends of these three.

PRINT: A scene or pattern applied to fabric with ink.

SCALE: On a floor plan the conversion standard that translates an object's true dimensions to its smaller representation. In fabric, the general size of a pattern's repeated elements.

SCHEME: Typically refers to a collection of colors in a particular space. Can also mean an assemblage of other elements, such as patterns or furniture.

SILHOUETTE: The outline of an object; its shape.

SLIPCOVER: A sewn fabric cover that slips over furniture to protect the underlying piece or to change the object's color or silhouette.

SOFFIT: The visible underside of an exposed structural element, such as a ceiling beam.

STUCCO: Textured plaster used to cover interior and exterior walls.

SUBWAY TILE: White rectangular tile often used as a backsplash or in baths. Usually 6 inches in length and 2 to 3 inches tall and laid out in a horizontal bricklike pattern. First used in turn-of-the-century subways, then in homes in the following decades.

SWAG: The downward swooping portion of a drapery.

TAPE: Flat, woven fabric ribbon used to embellish furniture and draperies.

TESTER: A full canopy, usually hanging over a bed.

TICKING: Striped cotton fabric originally used to cover pillows and mattresses. Typically a gray-blue and white, but for decorative purposes can span the color wheel.

TINT: The lighter, less intense values of a color. For instance: light blue, pale green, and soft pink.

TOILE: A printed pattern of a pastoral scene that appears on fabric. Typically appears in one or two colors on a contrasting background. Originated in France during the 18th century.

TÔLE: Painted metal accessories, such as trays.

TONE: The darker values of a color. For instance: indigo, emerald, and crimson.

TREADS: The footrests on a staircase.

TUDOR: Dominant decorative style of late 15th to early 16th century Britain that followed the Gothic period. While the latter was generally bare and imposing, the Tudor era saw increased ornamentation and more attention to secondary and private rooms.

TUFTED: Indentations on a surface that are sometimes marked with buttons. Typically seen on upholstered furniture, decorative pillows, and vintage mattresses.

TWILL: A weave that forms a pattern of diagonal, parallel lines.

UNDERTONE: An underlying color that can be read beneath its dominating tone.

UPHOLSTERY: Cushioned furniture that is covered with fabric.

VALANCE: The short, horizontal portion of drapery used to frame the top of a window or a canopy bed. Can be used for decorative purposes alone or to conceal hardware.

VALUE: How light or dark a color is.

VENEER: A thin sheet of wood glued to another surface for decorative purposes. Usually the finer or more interesting grain covers a less attractive base material.

WAINSCOT: Wooden paneling that covers the lower portion of a room's walls for decorative purposes.

WALLPAPER SIZING: Solution applied to walls to help the adherence of the wallcovering.

WARM COLORS: Colors with red or yellow undertones that create a warm impression and feeling. Can make a space feel cozy.

WELTING: Cord trim that covers seams on upholstered furniture.

WICKER: Hardy dried plant matter woven in a basketlike fashion to create furniture and accessories. Traditionally appears in outdoor settings, such as porches and patios. Modern versions can be made of all-weather synthetics.

dare to dream
be **inspired** and make your dream a reality

Better Homes and Gardens.
color schemes *made easy*

Better Homes and Gardens.
COLOR WITH CONFIDENCE

Better Homes and Gardens.
decorative paint techniques & ideas

GREAT **KIDS' ROOMS** COLLECTION

GREAT **WINDOWS & WALLS** COLLECTION

{ STYLE and INSPIRATION combine to bring you the best design ideas.
Look for these inspiring titles where home improvement books are sold.